Auditioning
for the
Musical
Theatre

Auditioning for the Musical Theatre

Fred Silver

Newmarket Press
New York

To my mother and father

First Edition
1 2 3 4 5 6 7 8 9 0

Library of Congress Cataloging in Publication Data

Silver, Fred.
Auditioning for the musical theatre.

Includes index
1. Singing—Instruction and study. 2. Singing—
Auditions. 3. Acting—Auditions. 4. Musical revue,
comedy, etc. I. Title.
MT820.S657 1985   782.81'07'1   84-29620
ISBN 0-937858-49-8
85- 13 2389

Quantity Purchases
Companies, professional groups, clubs, and other organizations may
qualify for special terms when ordering quantities of this title. For
information, contact the Special Sales Department, Newmarket Press,
3 East 48th Street, New York, New York 10017. Phone (212) 832-3575.

Designed by Deborah Daly

Manufactured in the United States of America

Contents

Foreword

As a pianist and vocal coach, and then as a composer (*Annie, Applause, Bye Bye Birdie, Golden Boy*), I've probably witnessed more auditions in the musical theatre than most people.

One inescapable fact about them: they last an average of 55 seconds.

Another fact (this, escapable, unfortunately): everyone listening to your audition wants, passionately, to like you. They may be bored, hungry, or even of a different sexual persuasion, but be sure: everyone is there for one reason—to cast the musical interestingly, lovingly, and, of course, successfully.

The problem is (and that is why Fred Silver's book is so invaluable): How do we slow down those 55 seconds so that we may control them and appear lovable, articulate, talented, handsome, or whatever?

Well, it's hard to appear talented if you're not. But appearing confident is not all that difficult, and confidence is a factor of talent.

You *appear* confident if you are correctly groomed (notice I don't say "well groomed") for the occasion. You *appear* confident if you speak or sing to someone as if that someone were intelligent and perceptive.

You *appear* confident if you know what you're doing—your music written out correctly for the pianist, your beginning attitude rehearsed, your song (most important!) deeply committed to memory.

These are all "things to do," and with things-to-do those 55 seconds are in your control.

That's why I tout this book. It's about things to do.

(By the way, if you appear confident and talented, you're beautiful, too!)

Charles Strouse

Introduction

Six years ago, when I started writing the "Audition Doctor" column for *Back Stage*, one of New York's most prestigious theatrical publications, I never dreamed it would be as popular and successful as it has been. It was as a result of writing the column, and answering so many questions from students in the musical performance classes that I've taught for twenty-five years, that the need for this book was driven home to me. Most actors and actresses gain their education about performing and auditioning for musicals in much the same way they got their first sexual insights—either through trial and error, or through the misinformation of their peers. This book attempts to correct that misinformation and reduce the trial and error to a minimum.

In this age, when there are fewer and fewer jobs available for more and more actors, it is an unfortunate fact that the American Musical is fast becoming a classical art form of the past, as expensive and impractical to produce as Grand Opera. Where we once had twenty to thirty new musical productions to look forward to each season, we now have only one, or two if we are lucky. It's obvious that only those with the greatest talent and the most readily identifiable skills are going to find employment in the musical theatre today.

Where do you go to learn these skills? Misinformation and hearsay from your peers are not going to do the trick. And unfortunately there are no universities or colleges, to my knowledge, where Musical Performance and Audition Technique for the Musical Theatre are taught. Although almost any school in the country has a fairly good theatre or drama program, the musical theatre is looked down upon as a bastard child, unworthy of the same consideration that is showered upon the "legitimate" theatre.

There are also very few books that teach musical audition skills; those that do exist are largely inaccessible, difficult to read, and even more difficult to comprehend.

It was for these reasons that I have shared in this book all that I've learned in the course of over twenty-five years of teaching actors how to audition, and accompanying them at many of their auditions.

In the chapters that follow, we are going to learn the techniques of acting a song and how to use subtext and monologues to make your performance of a song more believable. We are going to examine the construction of a song and take a look at its various parts. We'll discuss the voice in some detail, and the role of the voice teacher and vocal coach; we'll deal with stage fright and how to overcome it, learn how and what to do with the eyes and the arms, and discuss where and when to move during a performance. We will take a close look at the different types of songs that exist and learn which types are most suitable for musical theatre audition performances. We will even discover how to deal with accompanists so as not to be sabotaged at auditions.

What I have to teach is not that difficult, and I've written it with *you* in mind—whether you are an actor, singer, dancer, or aspiring to be any of these. It doesn't matter whether you are trying out for a Broadway show or for your high school or college musical; whether you are a professional or an amateur, whether you are putting together a cabaret act, or doing summer stock and regional theatre. There is something here to help everyone make the most of the skills they already possess, to kindle the desire to acquire those they haven't, and to show them how to go about it.

The musical audition classes that I give in New York City are packed with people at all different levels of talent and experience, from seasoned veterans to rank beginners. And even in this era when openings in the musical theatre are limited, a large majority of my students do find work in the business.

Finally, I would like to quote from the song "Getting to Know You" from *The King and I*, in which Oscar Hammerstein II writes that "When you become a teacher, by your pupils you'll be taught." I have been taught very well indeed by some of the most extraordinary students and friends that it has been my good fortune to know. It is to these past, present, and future musical audition students and friends that I dedicate this book.

1

The Audition

"Behold the Lord High Executioner"
The Mikado

If you were to tell an actor that he or she would be auditioning for a Broadway musical in the next few days, you would probably swear, from the reaction, that this was a fate worse than an IRS audit.

Successful actors with credits ranging from *Antigone* to *Zorba* become petrified at the thought of having to give a vocal audition. I have seen stars dissolve in tears at the prospect of having their work judged and found wanting. Once I had to shake and nearly throttle a world-famous actress who became hysterical backstage just before auditioning for Harold Prince and Stephen Sondheim for *Follies*. She was convinced that Mr. Prince hated her and had asked her to audition only so he could humiliate her. Of course this was not true.

The terror of having to put oneself on the line and face rejection can cause mental distress varying from mild stage fright to total emotional and physical collapse. Some performers give up in despair and vow never to be put in that thankless position again—while a few who have done their homework can't wait for the chance to show off their talents and skills.

What is there about the musical audition that makes it such a fearful prospect? Why are auditions necessary in the theatrical scheme of things? These questions have been haunting actors for ages, and I'm sure you'll agree that it's time for some straight answers. So let's examine what a musical audition really is.

The *American Heritage Dictionary of the English Language* defines an audition as "a presentation of something heard; a hearing, especially a trial hearing as that of an actor or musician." Obviously, we do not take that definition literally. If we did, I'm sure that auditions would have been taking place over the telephone for years.

Unfortunately for most of us, we are stuck with a word that doesn't begin to define what really happens during the auditioning process. An audition is so much more than a hearing. It is really more like a job interview—a one-sided interview in that they, the auditors, are allowed to ask anything within reason of you, but you are not allowed the same privilege.

At an audition, an actor trying out for a nonmusical can be expected to read from the script of the play he's up for. If it is a play that has been done before, and if the play is published, he can stage a fairly good reading by getting a copy from the library. If it is an original play that has never been produced before, and he is expected to give a "cold" reading, he is usually given a half hour to prepare. It is highly unlikely that he would be required to memorize his part; actors seldom memorize their lines until they are way into rehearsals. This, of couse, is because so much will change during the rehearsal period.

Contrast this with the actor/singer auditioning for a musical. He or she is not only expected to read from the script, but is expected to sing, and perform fully from memory, two staged musical numbers complete with gestures. In addition to this the actor/singer must be prepared to "move" for the choreographer. Although actor/singers are not expected to dance as well as dancers, they must move gracefully on stage. Dancers, on the other hand, although not expected to be the world's greatest actors (they usually are never asked to read unless speaking roles are being cast from the chorus), *are* expected to sing well and put over a song in believable fashion.

Obviously, auditioning for a musical requires not only all the skill and training that the actor has acquired through years of training, but it demands additional skills as well, some of them costing at least as much time, effort, money, and training as acting classes. The cost of years of voice lessons is monstrous, as is the cost of all the classes dancers must take in jazz, tap, modern, and ballet. Even actor/singers must invest in movement classes. Add to this the cost of a vocal coach and accompanist. All these are quite necessary if one wants to have a career in the musical theatre.

Yet despite the importance of all these requirements I've just outlined, I am constantly appalled by actors who have never sung, who when confronted with the opportunity to audition for a musical think nothing of rushing out to buy a copy of the latest hit, hiring a vocal coach for one or two sessions, and then finding an accompanist with whom they show up for a musical audition expecting to get immediate employment. Why do actors who have spent four years in college majoring in theatre, then come to New York and spent another couple of years taking scene study classes, commercial classes, sitcom or soap opera classes—all types of workshops and seminars—expect that musical audition and performance skills will somehow leap out of thin air and fasten onto them automatically? But I don't want to discourage you; getting to that state of preparedness is not as difficult as it might seem. You already know how to do the first important thing: act!

How many new skills you will need to develop depends on several factors: your age, your type, your area of specialization, your acting ability, your experience, and your vocal range and facility. If you are a character actor or actress, you may not be required to sing and dance as well as someone who is auditioning for the chorus. Ingenues always have to sing and dance well if they expect to work. Starring roles today demand only an actor with box office appeal. The Mermans and the Martins are, sadly, no longer required, although badly needed.

In fact, we can safely say that the more acting a part calls for, the less singing and dancing skills are needed. The only exceptions are shows that are dance oriented, such as *West Side Story, A Chorus Line,* and *On Your Toes.* As we get into the area of principal roles we find the vocal demands are much more easily satisfied. If the lead can carry a tune and be audible, the show is already way ahead. If Lauren Bacall can win two Tony awards for "best musical performance by an actress," then there is certainly hope for anyone. Therefore, I think it is foolish for an actor not to learn how to sing.

Getting the Right Basic Training

There are three steps that the nonsinging actor should take to enter the world of the musical theatre. First, he or she should find a good voice teacher, one who is sympathetic to building a healthy, robust singing voice that is an extension of the actor's speaking voice. It does little good if the singing voice is a magnificent, full, soaring instrument if the actor looks and talks nothing like that voice.

Jim Nabors, for example, has been blessed, or perhaps cursed, with a huge, full-bodied baritone that is completely at odds with the hillbilly twang that is his speaking voice. This is probably one reason he has never done a Broadway musical. The irony of the situation is that had he changed his speaking voice to match his singing voice he would be just another actor with a legitimate baritone voice. It is a bit late now for him to start singing in a high-pitched twang, and only character parts are written for voices like that.

This is one reason why it's important for the aspiring actor/singer to find a knowledgeable voice teacher, one who is quite familiar with the demands of the musical theatre and can be helpful in placing the actor's voice.

After working with a voice teacher and building up a workable instrument, the actor needs to link up with a good vocal coach, one who is proficient in teaching actors to sing the English language. This may seem ludicrous but it really is not. Voice teachers, in building the voice, vocalize their students only on open vowel sounds, to keep the throat open. They exhort their students to sing "on the vowel" only. English, however, is a language that is made up of consonants, compound consonants, plosives, fricatives, and liquid consonants, as well as dipthongs and tripthongs, and one of the vocal coach's tasks is to emphasize these other elements as well.

The vocal coach must also teach the singer to *phrase from the lyric*. The lyric, after all, is the script of the song—the part of the song that allows the actor to act. Since one doesn't speak in run-on sentences, there is no reason why one should sing them. Phrasing from the lyric, as opposed to phrasing from the music, allows the actor/singer to create the illusion that this is the first time his words have ever been felt, thought, and uttered.

The vocal coach also specializes in selecting the right audition material for his or her students. The vocal coach should have an extensive knowledge of the existing musical theatre repertoire. He or she should also be highly intuitive, making it possible to match actors with material that shows them off to best advantage. (In Chapter 9 I will discuss voice teachers and vocal coaches in more detail.)

Lastly, the actor needs to enroll and take part in an ongoing audition–performance class or workshop where he or she can get up each week in front of other actors and singers and mount songs. This is the only way to gain the confidence needed to go through the audition situation. It has been my experience that one can learn more by watching other people than one can learn in a private lesson. In the class one tends to learn what not to do by watching other people perform. If the technique looks good on others, the performer will most assuredly trust it on himself. In private lessons one has only the word of the teacher that the technique is working.

Special Pitfalls of the Musical Audition

A good audition, of course, is one that gets the job, yet there are many instances where brilliant auditions do not result in employment for the actors who gave them. To me, a good audition is one in which the performer, to the best of his abilities, reveals who and what he is as a human being while at the same time giving the auditors an idea of the extent of his talents. A bad audition is one in which the performer thoroughly confuses the people who are auditioning him by camouflaging himself with the wrong material and the wrong approach in presenting it.

First and always, it is important to remember that the reason that auditions are held in the first place is that someone has to hire someone else, and this is never an easy task. When a show is being cast there are definite requirements that have to be considered as to type, height, vocal ability and range, personality, and coloring. Even if these requirements are met by the actor, he or she is still up against others who may possess the very same qualifications. Actors are hired not because they are better than other people who are auditioning, but because they are more right for the part they are up for.

We have unfortunately been brought up in a competitive society, where since kindergarten we have been taught that being first and being best are everything. Although this may apply to games on the playing field, it doesn't apply in the theatre. In the theatre, actors are hired because they are right for the part. Everyone is an individual with his or her own specific talents. Success is so unpredictable; every actor has seen someone he feels is less qualified get a job he thought he should have gotten. Let's see why this happens in the musical audition situation.

In a straight, or legitimate, play (which is the unfortunate names given to non-musicals) you have a book or script that is approximately two and a half hours in length. A good director can take a halfway decent actor and create a believable performance easily. To bear this out let me take you back some years to two performances I saw of the Broadway production of the play *Butterflies Are Free*. When I first saw it Gloria Swanson (whom I later coached) was playing the role of the mother and Keir Dullea was playing her blind son. It was a lovely play—not tremendously deep but an enjoyable evening nonetheless. Keir Dullea was extremely moving as the blind son struggling for independence from his suburban Scarsdale mama.

About a year later I saw it again. This time I went because Rosemary Murphy, who was coaching with me, had taken over the role of the mother. When the curtain went up I was shocked. Kip Osborne, the former understudy, had now permanently replaced Keir Dullea in the role of the son. The opening scene, if you recall, reveals the son in his jockey shorts sitting on the bed in his new apartment, strumming a guitar, as Mama enters. Physically Mr. Osborne did not fit my conception of the character. He was extremely thin and had a protruding Adam's apple. When he started to speak I was sure this was going to be a terrible evening in the theatre, because his voice sounded like he was still going through puberty and hadn't changed yet.

Let me quickly tell you now that *I was completely wrong!* Mr. Osborne was marvelous. He gave a consummate performance and I was so taken with it and him that I gave him a standing ovation.

Why and how could this happen? Because he *is* an actor, because he had good direction, and because there was a great deal of character development that was written into the script. Because of all these things that he had going for him, he could become the boy.

In a musical this is not at all possible. Why? Because in a two-and-a-half hour musical there is at least an hour and a half of music and dance, which means that, after allowing for intermission, the book or script is at the most forty-five minutes in running time. In that brief period there is no time for character development. All the playwright can do is unfold the plot line.

Therefore, when directors are casting a musical and filling principal roles it is more important to them that the actor speak, move, sound, look, and feel like the character than be a brilliant actor, singer, or performer. That is why an unknown actress named Barbra Streisand got the role of a Jewish secretary from Brooklyn and stopped the show (*I Can Get It for You Wholesale*) with one minor comedy number that no one has sung since. That is also why an unknown actor who worked part-time as an elevator operator was able to audition for the part of Fiorello Laguardia in a major Broadway musical and get the *lead* in a show that would win the Pulitzer Prize. That elevator operator was Tom Bosley, and the show was *Fiorello!*

Why is this important? It means that just by being yourself you have a good chance for a callback or a reading if you are remotely close to what they are looking for. This is assuming that you do not obscure who you are by singing the wrong material and by playing someone you are not. Unfortunately most actors do not know how to play themselves. They have spent too many years playing other characters and it has become next to impossible for them to see themselves objectively.

Our primary concern is not to lose sight of the fact that what makes a song a theatrical experience, as opposed to primarily a musical one, is the acting of it. It is time to discuss the ways in which a song can be acted effectively in an audition or performance situation.

2

How To Act a Song

At an audition or during a performance it's essential to *act* a song if you want either to be considered for a job, or to keep the one you have already. Considering the hordes of actors who are "at liberty," just standing there and singing your way through a song is not only boring, it's insane. If you were to sing for me, I could tell within four measures or less if you could sing. It would take a bit longer for me to know if you could act. Sometimes after sitting through hours of auditioning actor/singers for a show I'm casting, I wonder why no one has thought of registering actor/singers and singer/dancers in several levels of proficiency, like nurses and engineers, or karate enthusiasts. Think how easy it would be if an ad in the trades said ". . . only third (most proficient) grade actor/singers will be considered."

Since this will probably never come about, the next best thing would be for actors, singers, and dancers to learn how to act *while* they are singing.

Those of you who are actors, or who have taken acting or scene study classes, will probably be angrily shaking your heads right now, saying "but I *do* act already, and I *know* that I am acting when I sing!" Do you really? Are you sure? Did you know that 90 percent of the actors who audition regularly for musicals stand there stiffly with their arms at their sides for an entire number? And of the remaining 10 percent, those who do use their arms tend to gesture spastically or nod their heads every time there is a downbeat or musical accent. Is that acting? Or else you'll see people standing there with their eyes rolling around inside their heads with no particular focus. Is that acting? Of course not! And yet many of these people are fine actors when they are involved in a straight, nonmusical scene. So what makes acting a song so different from acting a scene? One of the major differences is a little thing called timing.

To begin with, a scene is nearly always longer than a song, and it usually involves the dialogue of more than one person. In a song lyric, unless it's a duet, there is obviously only one person singing. More important, in a scene you are delivering dialogue in your own meter, your own individualized rhythm of speech. You speak in a tempo of your own choosing. You are not forced to speak in three-quarter or four-quarter time unless you are reading verse. You are not required to speak on pitch.

In a scene you are usually talking in the vernacular, unless you are acting something classical that is stylized. In a song, because the lyric is poetic, the content is terser and more concise. Thus the lyric requires a different sort of timing, one that allows the actor to act several beats *in advance* of what he is saying. It also requires the actor to elucidate more clearly his intent through the use of subtext. Since a lyric moves much more slowly than spoken dialogue, the audience is always going to be way ahead of the performer in anticipating his next words. Think back! Haven't we all, at one time or another, been totally bored by people who spoke so slowly that it seemed we had to wait an eternity for them to finish their sentences?

This invariably happens when the actor is singing a ballad. In a song that moves as slowly as a ballad does, the lyric falls behind the rhythm of speech. The remedy is not to act the lyric, but to invent a new text, one that is heard only by the actor, one made up of inner thoughts and emotions that sometimes can even be unrelated to the text. This new creative material we call *subtext*. Think of the "sub" in subtext not as meaning "below" the text, but "sub" as in substitution. In subtext we substitute thoughts, feelings, emotions, and even dialogue. We will discuss this in greater detail a little later.

Finally, and most important, in the lyric of a song there are spaces between words, and even larger spaces between complete thoughts and between sentences. It is during these spaces, or empty intervals of time, that the actor's performance dies and becomes lifeless. The actor in a song is *unfortunately* the slave of the piano player, since the pianist is in control of the tempo, or rate of speed in which the lyric can be delivered. So the actor is not even free to fill those spaces by rushing to the next word or sentence. This is one of the reasons actors avoid ballads and eagerly grab for up-tempo numbers. It stands to reason that the more words that are coming out of you, the less you have to do. That is why at many auditions you hear, ad nauseum, songs such as "Tonight at Eight," "I Met a Girl," "Luck Be a Lady Tonight," "They Call the Wind Mariah," "What I Did for Love," and "The Impossible Dream." Don't get me wrong, I think they're marvelous songs . . . just obvious choices that are far too overdone.

The other major factor that prevents actors from acting a song is how they use their eyes to spot. Spotting is the technique of where, how, and on whom to focus the eyes, and I cover it in detail in Chapter 4. It is used very differently in playing a scene than in acting a song. In a scene you are playing to another actor who is on stage with you. With a song you have to create the illusion that you are playing to an acting partner, who, unfortunately, is not at the audition with you (this is something we go into a great deal of detail about later on). Therefore in acting a song, the spot on which the actor would focus would have to be at the back of the house or rehearsal studio, to create the illusion that there is actually someone there.

I have noticed in my musical audition–performance classes that those students who are not playing to a specific (imaginary) acting partner usually wind up doing too much. They tend to use their arms and bodies spastically and they allow their bodies to be affected by the downbeats of the music they are listening to. Every time there is an accented beat or word their heads bob up and down. Sometimes the rhythmic accompaniment causes their torsos to move, ever so slightly, in time to the music. They are not aware of it, but they are upstaging themselves. The lack of an imaginary acting partner to focus on causes the body, perhaps subconsciously, to compensate for a lack of something that should be happening.

Those that do have a specific acting partner not only look better, they act better. In acting a song less is definitely more. So, the first rule of acting a song is *always have a specific acting partner or partners when you sing.*

Another important major difference between acting a scene and acting a song is that much more is required of the audience that is watching and listening to a song being performed than of one watching a dramatic scene. When we observe actors playing to one another in a scene, they are talking in a way we are used to hearing people talk. They are moving the way we are used to seeing people move, and they are expressing emotions we are used to seeing expressed, for the most part. On the other hand, when we are watching and listening to a vocal performance we are not only listening to the dramatic content of the lyric—we are also required to take in the melody, harmony, musical accompaniment, lyrical phrasing, and vocal quality as well. In addition, we must at the same time, watch the performer move, gesture, and act.

First Preparations

How, then, does one act a song? The first thing you have to do is to make exactly the same preparations you would make when acting a scene or a play, plus a little bit more.

STEP ONE

If you were involved in a play you would read it thoroughly and do an in-depth analysis of the character you would be portraying. You would know how old or young the character is. You would know everything there was to know about the motivations, desires, and needs of your character. Is a song any different? Not really. The lyric, after all, is a script, and if the emotions expressed in the lyric were not strong enough, or if the character implied by the lyric wasn't interesting enough, the song would not have been written in the first place. Be sure to know *why* the character you will be playing is making that particular statement, *what* the motivation and dramatic necessity of the scene defined by the lyric consists of, *where* the action is taking place, *when* it is happening (almost always in the now), and to *whom* it is being played.

After you have done an in-depth character analysis of the song and character, as defined by the lyric, you will be far ahead of nearly everyone else showing up to audition. The reason most people select the audition songs they wind up singing is that they have heard someone else sing them and they liked the performance and the song. The only thing that is wrong with this is that subconsciously they are going to give a second-hand performance—one that is influenced and based on what they have already seen and heard, not one that is the result of analysis and introspection. So please avoid that pitfall. Take the time and trouble and do your preparation and give a first-hand performance.

STEP 2

The second important step in preparing a song from scratch is to get a notebook, the composition type, and copy the lyric from the music in your notebook. Write it out as if it were your script. After all, if you were in a play you would take your script and would pencil in all entrances and exits and any stage business suggested by the director. You would probably note any subtextual ideas as well. It stands to reason that if you tried to do this on your music itself, no pianist would ever be able to read from it. Thus the admonition to copy it in your notebook. Be sure to leave two blank lines before each line, sentence, or complete thought of the lyric you are writing out. The two blank lines are very important, as we shall learn in the next step.

STEP 3

Remember when I said that an actor is alive only as long as he has dialogue coming out of him, or is involved in a physical and emotional life that is perceptible to the audience? Well, it's all too true. Since the actor, standing in place singing a song, is alive and interesting to watch only when words are coming out of him, he usually dies and ceases to be interesting in the spaces between lines. It is these spaces that have to be filled dramatically, and the way to fill them is to write additional dialogue and subtext in the two blank lines you have provided yourself with between parts of the lyric.

Here is an example of a slow-moving song, typical of an audition ballad. Note that it contains many pregnant pauses, the musical term for which is "air."

With a Song in My Heart

With a song in my heart *(air)*
I behold your adorable face. *(air)*
Just a song at the start, *(air)*
But it soon is a hymn to your grace. *(air)*
When the music swells *(air)*
I'm touching your hand; *(air)*
It tells that you're standing near *(air)* and *(air)*
At the sound of your voice *(air)*

"With a Song in My Heart," lyrics by Lorenz Hart, music by Richard Rodgers. © 1929 (Renewed) Warner Bros. Inc. All rights reserved. Used by permission.

Heaven opens its portals to me. *(air)*
Can I help but rejoice *(air)*
That a song such as ours came to be? *(air)*
But I always knew *(air)*
I would live life through *(air)*
With a song in my heart for you.

It is during these pauses that the performer dies. His dialogue is interrupted by musical fill and he loses the attention of his audience.

I'll never forget something that happened when I was under contract to Williamson Music, then part of Chappell, the largest publisher of show music in the world. The show *Funny Girl* was just about to go into rehearsals, and Barbra Streisand had just recorded the demo of "People," which was to become the show's hit ballad. Chappell was involved with publishing the score, and they played me the demo and asked for my opinion. It became readily apparent to me that nearly a third of the song was made up entirely of pauses (air) and held notes. It bothered me that the single-word title of the song was repeated eleven times, and that each time it was uttered it was followed by these extremely long pauses that would have to be filled on stage by some sort of acting device.

It turned out that I was only partially right in my assumption. At the preview I saw of *Funny Girl*, the audience was coughing and rattling programs during the pauses in Miss Streisand's performance of the song, and I felt the song, beautiful as it was, slowed the show down. Then a very interesting thing happened. No sooner did the recording of the song hit the airwaves and become a commercial hit than audiences started paying full attention and cheering. I learned that once a song becomes that familiar, the memory of your initial response to it, when hearing it outside of a theatrical context, elates you and creates the momentum needed to propel the song and the show along.

How then does the performer tackle pauses in audition

situations? To make all this a little less confusing, try to conceive of the lyric as being only partially written. After all, it only occupies 50 to 70 percent of the music it is sung over. Since 30 to 50 percent of the lyric is made up of rests and sustained notes, it is up to you to write and act additional dialogue or subtext. In writing it try not to create lines that are verbal; instead, choose lines that cause you to react emotionally and physically. Pepper them with lots of expletives. You know . . . colorful words like Damn! God! Gee! Wow! and preferably *lots* of the unprintable kind. Expletives create a sort of "instant acting pill" for you to take. They give you immediate and instant color, life, and vitality because they force you to react.

Another way to fill this empty space is to create a scene involving yourself and an acting partner. Actually, a song is always a scene between you and another acting partner or partners. A scene can be created in several different ways. First of all, your acting partner can be completely passive. There he or she is . . . just smiling at you benevolently as you go your merry way emoting your heart out. Yet in certain instances we can get a lot more mileage out of our acting partners. We can give them the extra dialogue that we were previously giving to ourselves. Of course, this will only work in certain songs where the lyric, acting as a script, permits it. I call this technique *active* because the acting partner, now a participant in the dialogue, has an active life. The former technique I have named *passive* because the acting partner just stands there passively nodding his or her head in agreement with everything we say.

The last acting technique employing the lyric to create a script as the basis for a musical performance I call *stage directions*. With this technique the actor overwrites stage directions the way an overzealous playwright might. They give the actor some sort of direction to follow, and they work best when they describe emotional responses, physical reactions, and movements. They would be played during the air or empty spaces between lines.

To make the three techniques that I have just discussed a little clearer, here are some examples of how they can be used.

Acting Technique 1: Passive

I Get a Kick Out of You

(verse)
My story is much too sad to be told,
But practically everything leaves me totally cold.
The only exception I know is the case
When I'm out on a quiet spree
Fighting vainly the old ennui,
And I suddenly turn and see
Your fabulous face.

(chorus)
I get no kick from champagne,
Mere alcohol doesn't thrill me at all,
So tell me why should it be true
That I get a kick out of you?

Some get a kick from cocaine
I'm sure that if I took even one sniff
It would bore me terrific'ly too.
Yet I get a kick out of you.

I get a kick ev'ry time I see
You're standing there before me.
I get a kick tho' it's clear to me
You obviously don't adore me.

I get no kick in a plane,
Flying too high with some guy in the sky
Is my idea of nothing to do.
Yet I get a kick out of you.

"I Get a Kick Out of You" is typical of the brilliance of Cole Porter. Unfortunately, Porter usually wrote about people who hardly exist anymore. Most of his heros and heroines lived out their lives on Sutton Place, Park Avenue, or Beekman Place. They spent their summers in Oyster Bay or Newport, wintered on the Riviera, and never had to work a day in their lives. Some of the songs are just as vibrant today as the day they were written, but they present a problem to the actor/singer in that the language of the lyric, and the similes and metaphors, are not what the average actor has in his or her vocabulary. Also, many actors lack the chic and elegance to make these songs believable. To sing and act songs such as these, we need to employ some sort of subtextual technique.

The reason we have chosen the passive technique for this song is that it is very clear that the man who sings, or I should say acts, it doesn't need anyone interrupting him. Since the scene is self-contained, the first choice to be made would be who is the acting partner? Obviously, in this case it is the girl he is in love with (or if the singer is a woman, the man she loves). In the case of other songs, the acting partner will not be so readily apparent—it might be the singer's best friend, his shrink, or even a stranger. One very important thing to bear in mind is that we are different people with different acting partners. You're not the same with your parents as you are with your boss, so choose wisely.

You might find yourself thinking when you analyze some songs, "But the singer could just as easily be talking to himself. Why do I need an acting partner for this song?" The answer to that is one *always* needs an imaginary acting partner when playing a song because the audience subconsciously identifies with, and vicariously becomes, the acting partner. If there is no acting partner to begin with, you will never have the full attention of your audience. It is very difficult for an audience to focus its attention on someone who is talking to himself. On some level, this makes us feel uncomfortable.

Here is how the passive technique works with each line of subtext written and acted in advance of each corresponding thought and idea of the lyric.

(*verse*)
(*Bob, looking very dejected, turns to his fiancée, Denise,*
and says:) *Denise. I don't know what's happening to me.*
My story is much too sad to be told,
Nothing seems to be the same anymore.
But practically everything leaves me totally cold.
How? Well, for one thing, I don't seem to sleep as well as
I used to.
The only exception I know is the case
Also, I just sort of sit around and kill time.
When I'm out on a quiet spree
I don't seem to be interested in the things that used to
turn me on.
Fighting vainly the old ennui,
I know this may sound ridiculous
And I suddenly turn and see
but I'm only comfortable when I'm with you.
Your fabulous face.
(*Bob walks downstage toward Denise and continues:*)
For example, I don't go to hockey games anymore
I get no kick from champagne,
Yes, I know that I was always an Islanders fanatic
Mere alcohol doesn't thrill me at all,
but the last few times I left after thirty minutes.
So tell me why should it be true
Hockey just bores me now.
That I get a kick out of you?
(*scratching his head:*)
You know how much I love playing poker with the guys.
Some get a kick from cocaine
Lately when they call me I make up some story or other to
get out of it.
I'm sure that if I took even one sniff
I just don't seem to find their jokes funny anymore.
It would bore me terrific'ly too.
(*He nervously moves to the side as he says:*)

You know, there's only one person I seem to feel comfortable with these days.
Yet I get a kick out of you.
You!
I get a kick ev'ry time I see
I really look forward to taking long walks with you.
You're standing there before me.
I can't wait till I pick you up at your house just to go for a drive
I get a kick tho' it's clear to me
or maybe go to a movie.
You obviously don't adore me.
(He paces back to center and finally admits to her)
Look, I know we agreed to wait one more year till I graduated from law school,
I get no kick in a plane,
but I don't even know if I'm gonna finish law school if things keep up this way.
Flying too high with some guy in the sky
I can't concentrate on my studies. All I do is think about wanting to be with you.
Is my idea of nothing to do.
Put me out of my misery and say that we'll get married as soon as possible.
Yet I get a kick out of you.

Using the passive technique in this manner makes it easier for the actor/singer to play a song in a more realistic fashion than by merely using the lyric as a script. First of all, he is playing himself, acting and moving the way he would in a real-life situation. After all, isn't the classic definition of acting "responding to an imaginary situation as if it were happening in real life"? The other gift it imparts to the actor is an originality of performance. No one can possibly copy what he has done because they can't get inside his mind. The song and performance are his and have his trademark on them.

Let's see how the passive technique works with another song. This one is a poignantly beautiful ballad by Jerry Herman from the Broadway musical *Dear World*.

And I Was Beautiful

He stood and looked at me
And I was beautiful
For it was beautiful
How he believed in me.
His love was strong enough
To make me anything,
So I was everything
He wanted me to be.

But then he walked away
And took my smile with him,
And now the years blur by,
But every now and then
I stop and think of him
And how he looked at me,
And all at once
I'm beautiful again,
For a moment,
I'm beautiful again.

If we analyze the lyric, knowing nothing about the character who originally sang the song in the show, we can deduce the following:

1. It can only be sung by a woman.

2. The song is about an event that took place in her past.

3. In some way she would like to relive that experience.

4. The song is a narration, i.e., she is telling a story.

5. During the telling of her story she is reliving the past, but by the end of the song she has to return to the present reality of who and what she is.

6. She is a very sensitive and vulnerable person capable of intense feeling.

Here is how her subtext might read if it were written out. In this particular example, her acting partner might be anyone she chose to confide in—her therapist, best friend, even her own child.

> *The person I'll always remember the most, as long as I live, is my grandfather.*
> **He stood and looked at me**
> *I was his princess, his pride and joy.*
> **And I was beautiful**
> *In his eyes I could do no wrong.*
> **For it was beautiful how he believed in me.**
> *My parents weren't even allowed to punish me if he was around.*
> **His love was strong enough to make me anything**
> *Just one stern look of disappointment or disapproval from him and I never disobeyed again.*
> **So I was everything he wanted me to be.**
> *I was about eight or nine when he got cancer.*
> **But then he walked away**
> *They wouldn't let me see him the last few months of it. He didn't want me to see him shrunken up and in pain.*
> **And took my smile with him,**
> *His funeral was the first one I ever went to.*
> **And now the yeas blur by,**
> *I guess I got over it, but his passing left a big, empty hole in my life.*

But every now and then
After that, when I prayed to God I would imagine that
God looked just like my grandfather.
I stop and think of him
Do you know what? . . . I still do.
And how he looked at me
Whenever I'm frightened or in a bind I call his name.
And all at once
Something fantastic happens!
I'm beautiful again.
I'm no longer frightened or confused.
For a moment,
I get this strange sense of peace,
I'm beautiful
and I know, somehow, he's there.
Again.

Acting Technique 2: Active

Let's go to our next example, the active technique, where instead of giving the extra dialogue we are writing to ourselves, we give it to our acting partner. I have chose one of my own songs, entitled "This Is My Last Show," which is a good example of what an audition song should do—make the audience care about the person who is singing it.

After analyzing the lyric it is apparent that in this song our scene takes place backstage in a darkened, empty theatre. The stage is bare except for a worklight. A young actress is seated, totally alone, when a stagehand walks in. He seems to be the most appropriate acting partner for this song.

In the active technique it is the responses—emotional, physical, and verbal—to your imaginary acting partner's probing, goading, or concern that gives you your own acting life.

This Is My Last Show

The cast are all at parties
At Backstage or at Sardi's
To celebrate our closing night.
But why this exaltation
And all this celebration?
To me it's a barbaric rite.

My grief is private
So like a jerk
I'm in this theatre where I
Used to work.

While others are out drinking
I'm sitting here and thinking.
Thinking of my closing night.

(chorus)
Is it strange how silence seems to fill
The air now.
Why this sudden sadness I cannot define?
All my things are gone. The dressing room seems
Bare now;
Just empty wall with tacks . . .
Where posters hid the cracks.

Faces I expect to see come back to haunt me.
If I can hear their laughter,
Why can't I hear mine?
Guess it's time to own up finally
This ingenue has grown up finally.
And now it's time to go.

Something tells me so.
Now at last I know
This is my last show.
Maybe till the next time
If there is a next time.
But will there be a next time? I don't know.

Since this is now a scene involving two people who both have dialogue, the lyric and inserts will have to be written out as a script. We are going to call the acting partner Pops. Pops is in his sixties, a pipe-smoking, fatherly man who is the doorman/ custodian of the empty theater in which this scene is taking place. Becuase we are using the active technique, Pops has to have the first line. The young girl who is singing we will call Cindy.

POPS:
Cindy! . . . What on earth are you doing here all alone?
CINDY:
The cast are all at parties
POPS:
Where are they?
CINDY:
At Backstage or at Sardi's
To celebrate our closing night.
POPS:
Why aren't you with them, dear?
CINDY:
But why this exaltation
And all this celebration?
To me it's a barbaric rite.
POPS:
Closing night parties are a tradition, Cindy. You really should be with everyone else. After all, you've spent six months in a show with them.

CINDY:
My grief is private
So like a jerk
I'm in this theatre
Where I used to work.
POPS:
I still think you should be with them. After all they are
your friends. They'll be hurt by your absence. Besides,
what good is being here going to do you?
CINDY:
While others are out drinking
I'm sitting here and thinking.
POPS:
But about what?
CINDY:
Thinking of my closing night.
(She walks downstage toward Pops.)
POPS:
This place sure seems like a morgue now.
CINDY:
(Agreeing with him.)
Is it strange how silence seems to fill the air now.
POPS:
I'm sure gonna miss you. You promise to come and visit
me once in a while?
CINDY:
(Shaking her head to indicate she will.)
Why this sudden sadness I cannot define?
POPS:
Do you have all your stuff? Do you want to check the
dressing room, in case you've forgotten something?
CINDY:
(Indicating that there is no need to.)
All my things are gone. The dressing room seems
bare now,
POPS:
It sure doesn't look the same, does it?

CINDY:
Just empty wall with tacks
Where posters hid the cracks.
POPS:
Cindy, what are you going to remember most about this place?
CINDY:
Faces I expect to see come back to haunt me.
POPS:
Well, I hope they'll be happy memories.
CINDY:
If I can hear their laughter, why can't I hear mine?
POPS:
Do you have any plans for the future?
CINDY:
Guess it's time to own up finally
This ingenue has grown up finally.
(She turns slightly, preparing to leave, but changes her mind.)
And now it's time to go.
Something tells me so.
Now at last I know
This is my last show.
POPS:
Cindy, you're being too dramatic. I bet you'll be working again within a few weeks.
CINDY:
(Trying to bolster up her spirits.)
Maybe till the next time,
POPS:
Of course there's going to be a next time!
CINDY:
If there is a next time.
POPS:
You know, you could always go back to school . . . But, you don't want to do that.

CINDY:
(Shaking her head no.)
But will there be a next time?
POPS:
Take care of yourself, Cindy. I gotta get back to work.
(He waves good-bye.)
CINDY:
(Half reaching out to him to wave good-bye.)
I don't know.
(She turns, and exits slowly while holding the last note.)

The advantage of the active technique is that using an acting partner to play off gives the actor a relaxed believability that is very rare in a musical audition situation. The actor can *be* more and *do* less. The disadvantage of the active technique is mainly that the actor is limited by the dialogue he has created for the acting partner. In the passive technique the actor has greater freedom in inventing suitable dialogue as well as more choices to make in selecting an appropriate acting partner, a scene for the song to take place in, and a more dynamic subtext. With the right song, however, the active technique can be dynamite.

Here is a Rodgers & Hart classic that comes to life only through the prodding questioning of the acting partner. It works perfectly with the active technique, yet it would not be as successful with a passive acting partner.

Have You Met Miss Jones

(verse)
It happened! I felt it happen.
I was awake, I wasn't blind.
I didn't think. I felt it happen.

Now I believe in matter over mind.
And so you see we mustn't wait.
The nearest moment that we marry
Is too late.

(*chorus*)
"Have you met Miss Jones,"
Someone said as we shook hands.
She was just Miss Jones to me.
Then I said, "Miss Jones,
You're a girl who understands
I'm a man who must be free."

Then, all at once I lost my breath,
And all at once, was scared to death,
And all at once I owned the earth
And sky.

Now, I've met Miss Jones,
And we'll keep on meeting till we die.
Miss Jones and I.

The lyric to any theatrical audition song presents several problems when viewed out of context of its original setting within the confines of a musical libretto.

1. We have no idea who the character is, what he does for a living, how old he is, where he comes from, how much he makes.

2. We have no idea who the actor is talking to, and why that particular acting partner was chosen in the first place.

3. What time span does the song encompass? Is the actor talking about something that happened five minutes ago, yesterday, a month ago; or is it happening right now?

"Have You Met Miss Jones" presents the actor/singer with the difficulty of having the verse to the song occur in the present and the chorus occur, at least narratively, in the past. Choosing the right acting partner, and giving him the right dialogue, can make the actor relive the past as if it were happening again, right now. Using the active technique, I have chosen two college roommates as our participants in this scene. We'll call them Gary and Frank.

> *(It is four o'clock in the morning. Gary has just returned from a date. Frank sits bolt upright and says:)*
> FRANK:
> *Gary, it's 4 A.M. Where the hell have you been?*
> GARY:
> *(Elated and excited.)*
> **It happened!**
> FRANK:
> *Have you lost your bird, or something? What are you talking about?*
> GARY:
> **I felt it happen.**
> FRANK:
> *How do you know?*
> GARY:
> **I was awake, I wasn't blind.**
> **I didn't think. . . .**
> FRANK:
> *In your state of hysteria how could you be certain of anything?*
> GARY:
> **I felt it happen.**
> **Now I believe in matter over mind.**
> FRANK:
> *Gary, for Christ's sake calm down!*
> GARY:
> **And so you see we mustn't wait.**

FRANK:
(Very exasperated.)
I still haven't an inkling of what you're talking about.
GARY:
The nearest moment that we marry is too late.
FRANK:
(Beginning to see the light.)
*Aha, so you met someone. Why don't you calm down and
tell me about it. Start at the very beginning.*
GARY:
(Moving downstage and collecting himself.)
"Have you met Miss Jones,"
Someone said as we shook hands.
FRANK:
How did you feel about her? Was the chemistry there?
GARY:
(Shaking his head no.)
She was just Miss Jones to me.
FRANK:
Then what did you do?
GARY:
Then I said, "Miss Jones, you're a girl who
Understands I'm a man who must be free."
FRANK:
*Boy, that was telling her. I bet she didn't stand a chance.
How did she react to that?*
GARY:
Then all at once I lost my breath.
FRANK:
It looks like she scared the hell out of you.
GARY:
And all at once was scared to death.
FRANK:
I bet it must have been pretty wonderful.
GARY:
(Nodding his head in agreement.)

And all at once I owned the earth and sky.
FRANK:
Do you think it could lead to something serious?
GARY:
Now I've met Miss Jones
And we'll keep on meeting till we die,
FRANK:
Does this mean that I'm going to have to shop for a new
roommate soon?
GARY:
(Nodding his head affirmatively.)
Miss Jones and I.

Acting Technique 3: Stage Directions

In this last technique, based on the lyric, we are going to emulate the kind of playwright who continually overwrites stage directions. I have seen plays where the directions were longer than the text, for example:

(Agatha nervously enters the room, turning every moment or so to look over her shoulder as if she's been followed. Anxiety ripples over her as she wipes beads of perspiration from her forehead. She clears her throat, turns, becomes startled to see George there and says:)
AGATHA:
Excuse me, I was looking for my purse.

Something similar happens when we use this technique with a song. I formulated it for people who, like myself, respond well to descriptions and suggestions. For this example we will use a song by Murray Grand from *New Faces of 1952* that's become a classic.

Guess Who I Saw Today, My Dear?

(verse)
You're so late getting home from the office.
Did you miss your train?
Were you caught in the rain?
No, don't bother to explain.
Can I fix you a dry martini?
As a matter of fact, I'll have one with you
For to tell you the truth I've had quite a day too.

(chorus)
Guess who I saw today, my dear?
I went to town to buy the kids a thing or two,
And thought I'd stop to have a drink when I was
through.
I looked around for some place near
And found a most attractive French cafe and bar.
It really wasn't very far.

The waiter showed me to a dark secluded corner
And when my eyes became accustomed to the
gloom
I saw two people at the bar who were so much in
love
That even I could see it clear across the room.

Guess who I saw today, my dear?
I've never been so shocked before.
I headed blindly towards the door.
They didn't see me passing through.
Guess who I saw today?
I saw you!

"Guess Who I Saw Today, My Dear?" lyrics and music by Murray Grand and Elise Boyd. Copyright R. C. Jay Publishing Corp. Used by permission.

Now, here are the stage directions for this song.

(Amanda looks up nervously as George enters. She is slightly flushed. She nervously says:)
You're so late getting home from the office.
(She starts to fidget with her hair.)
Did you miss your train?
(Looking slightly away from him she continues:)
Were you caught in the rain?
(She interrupts him just as he's about to answer.)
No, don't bother to explain.
(Suddenly she's very solicitous of him. She says cordially:)
Can I fix you a dry martini?

(. . . becoming her charming self once more she gaily smiles and says:)
As a matter of fact, I'll have one with you
(Tossing her head, she says:)
For to tell you the truth I've had quite a day too.
(Amanda walks downstage toward him smiling with just a bit too much warmth for believability.)
Guess who I saw today, my dear?
(Trying to justify herself she says:)
I went to town to buy the kids a thing or two,
(She casually picks some lint off her sleeve.)
And thought I'd stop to have a drink when I was through.
(Completely deadpan, she says:)
I looked around for some place near
And found a most attractive French cafe and bar.
(Reassuring him that everything is all right.)
It really wasn't very far.
(Amanda becomes more involved in the telling of her story.)
The waiter showed me to a dark secluded corner
And when my eyes became accustomed to the gloom

(She becomes misty-eyed.)
I saw two people at the bar who were so much in
love
That even I could see it clear across the room.
(Little by little she starts to react emotionally.)
Guess who I saw today, my dear?
(She clutches at her throat.)
I've never been so shocked before.
(She grasps her hands together.)
I headed blindly towards the door.
(With great agitation and pain she exclaims:)
They didn't see me passing through.
*(She tries to regain her composure and lighten the facade
she is presenting to George.)*
Guess who I saw today?
*(After a long beat, bitterness is etched in her face as her
hands and body tense up. She looks at him, delivers the
next line.)*
I saw you!
*(She looks down. After a moment the tension drains out
of her and she is left limp.)*

Of the three techniques, that of stage directions is probably
the easiest for the trained actor. After all, he has worked with
directors all of his acting career, and stage directions are something he is used to if he has read plays of any consequence.
This technique can be combined with either of the other two.
As a matter of fact, any combination of the three techniques
may be used at any time in any song.

Acting Technique 4: The Monologue— Dramatic Counterpoint

There is still one acting technique that we haven't discussed,
which, when combined with a song, can create a totally new

entity that allows the actor's performance to be as good, in quality, as the song. This technique entails the creation of an original monologue by the actor. This monologue has nothing at all to do with the lyric or content of the song, although the central essence or theme of the monologue is directly derived from the central essence or subject of the lyric. Just as one could capsulize Shakespeare's *Macbeth* by saying that the central essence of it deals with blind ambition and the retribution that comes from immoral thirst for power, one can find a central essence in the plot or situation drawn in any song.

This is a complicated and sophisticated technique, and I make it optional in my classes for those students who really need to create believable performances. Because it requires such creative work and concentration on the part of the actor, not many performers are willing to master the intricacies of the technique. I like to call it dramatic counterpoint because I think it is to acting what counterpoint is to musical composition. Where as harmony deals with the vertical relationship of notes to one another to form chords bound to the melodic structure of a melody, counterpoint is the art of creating two melodies which, although independent of one another, still function together to create a new, more complex piece of music wherein the sum is greater than the parts.

The monologue technique does exactly that. The song and the monologue are taking place simultaneously; the monologue is being acted, but is experienced, at least consciously, only by the performer. The lyric of the song is heard by the audience, who are unaware that the freedom and originality that seem to come from the actor are really born out of a script entirely of his own making. Once it is explained, step by step, this technique will become not only understandable but a joyful, challenging acting experience.

Invariably when I explain and assign this technique in my class, to specific actors who need it, loud cries and groans of protest fill the room. It always amuses me to find that once an actor successfully writes, performs, and fuses his monologue with a song, he is "hooked." From that time on it requires the greatest persuasion from me to get them to go back to simpler techniques.

The monologue technique should be considered when any of the following criteria are met:

1. The song you are singing is one that has been over-exposed. Everybody knows it, and you want to get a fresh handle on it; a new way of performing it.

2. The lyrics to the song are not in today's vernacular. The lyrics are either very poetic, or they are archaic, and it would embarrass you to act what the lyric means if you performed it as written.

3. The song is so well written that it "wipes you out." This would most likely happen if you were singing a Sondheim song or something of that complexity. In songs such as these everything is spelled out in the lyric. There is no room for subtext to be derived from the lyric because the lyric itself is a form of subtext to begin with. The danger of a song being too good is that its brilliance may up-stage you. It is the song, not your performance of it, that will be remembered by the people you audition for.

4. You are forced to sing a song that you don't relate to and that has lyrics you hate. This may often happen to you in a show when you have to make a number work that you despise. If you don't they will most certainly replace you in the show.

5. The song is simple and the lyrics lack much dramatic content. Even so, it is beautiful enough to warrant your singing it, and you want a dramatic performance to compensate for the blandness of the lyric.

If you find that any of these situations is present, the mono-logue technique of dramatic counterpoint can be a useful way out. The technique requires several steps that *must* be followed exactly. Skip one and you're in a lot of trouble. I have found from experience in teaching my performance classes that actors who are too ambitious and eager to rush ahead are the ones who skip one of the steps. They want the power that the use of the monologue technique gives, yet think they can shortcut the process. Unfortunately, shotcutting in this technique only causes failure and frustration, so do follow the steps exactly.

Learning this technique is like juggling several oranges. We have to start with one and gradually add the others until finally all the oranges are up in the air operating at the same time.

We are now ready to construct a monologue for a song, and I have chosen for our first example a song I wrote, entitled "Someone in My Life." Our first step is to analyze the lyric.

Someone in My Life

(verse)
Sometimes I feel such a desolation;
Words cannot convey . . .
The quiet, lonely desperation
That never goes away.

I'm like a playground no one plays in,
A haunted house that no one stays in,
A vacant church that no one prays in
Empty and unused.
Is it any wonder I'm confused.

(chorus)
I need someone in my life
When these empty feelings stab at me.
I need someone to inhabit me.
Someone in my life.

I need someone in the void
Of my sleeping and my waking hours
Who can end the angry, waking hours.
Someone in my life.

Someone in my world . . .
For my world's begun to reek of night.
Someone . . . who'll be the sun,
Not just a satellite.

There's a famine in my life.
I need someone who can end this drought;
Bring the gentle rain I've done without
So I can see the grain grow.
So I can be a rainbow.

Someone to make me whole,
Who'll occupy my soul.
Someone! . . .
Anyone! . . .
Someone! . . .
Someone in my life.

Both the lyric and the music to this song have an unfulfilled, romantically restless quality about them. The character who sings the song is going through his or her "dark night of the soul." If we had to cull some central essence from the lyrical content it would most likely be about being unfulfilled and feeling totally unwanted and unneeded. It would be very difficult for any actor to make this statement at an audition without feeling stripped naked emotionally in front of the people he or she was auditioning for. Obviously some subtextual device is needed—one that makes it safe for the actor to play a situation or emotion that is as threatening as the one implied by this lyric, yet safe enough to hide behind at an audition. If the actor sang (acted) this song as written, it would be a physically stagnant performance. Most likely there would be very few original choices made about what to do with the arms and the hands.

The actor would also be confused about where and when to move. The monologue solves these problems.

I gave this song to one of my students, Sandy, and this is what she came up with. Here is the gist of our discussion of her monologue preparation.

SANDY: First of all I think that the character in the song is going through her "dark night of the soul." I think she is suffering extraordinary pain.

F.S.: I agree, but who could she possibly be that open to in telling about what she is experiencing? Who could her acting partner be?

SANDY: Her best friend?

F.S.: No! If she talked this way to her best friend she wouldn't have her for long. We tend to spare our friends the real garbage that is in our lives. I think it should be her psychotherapist. Shrinks make the best acting partners. You can tell them anything and everything without the risk of their subjectivity, or of their rejection.

SANDY: Good idea! Should my monologue be about loneliness and desperation? What I mean is, should I paraphrase the lyric of the song?

F.S.: Absolutely not! The whole purpose of the monologue is to get away from the limitations of having to say words or play a scene that is self-threatening. What situation have you experienced that makes you feel as vulnerable as the character in the song does, and yet is safe enough for you to admit to us in class?

SANDY: Well, as you know, I quit smoking two months ago; the same day I joined Overeaters Anonymous. Those next two days were really hell for me. I mean, I would have killed for a cigarette and a piece of cheesecake. I think I am going to use that as my subtext and subject for the monologue.

(Sandy came in the following week with a memorized monologue which went as follows:)

Dr. Korngold ... thanks so much for seeing me on such short notice. ... I don't know what I would have done if I couldn't have gotten an appointment. . . . Things have been really lousy the past couple of days.

It's the compulsive eating. It's gotten considerably worse. (Wringing her hands) I just can't stop the binging. (Shaking her head) I've never been out of control like this. (Looking frightened) When did it start? . . . last week . . . right after my graduation from "Smokequitters."

Yes, I know there is a connection, Dr. Korngold, but knowing there is a connection and ending the connection are two different things (Beat) . . . Doctor! Is it really necessary for you to smoke during our session? . . . Yes, I *know* you enjoy smoking and that you don't have the problem . . . but (Hesitating) . . . Jesus H. Christ! Right now I could kill for a cigarette.

Why? . . . Well, it's either that or a cheese danish, and the cheese danish is fattening and not very practical right now. Damn it! . . . I'm addicted to nicotine. Isn't that reason enough? I mean the food makes the pain go away and the cigarette helps me to forget I ever had the pain to begin with.

No, doctor! . . . I do not want to trace it back to early childhood. I don't think it's important. It's my session and I don't, absolutely don't want to go back into that garbage. All I want is a cigarette. So please let me have one.

My God! You can't mean that you're not going to let me have one! I'm desperate. (Getting more and more upset) I am not going to play by your rules. This is grossly unfair. Here I am having a nicotine fit and you're trying to tell me it's for my own good.

(Suddenly quiet) Doctor, I want a cigarette, I need a cigarette . . . and if you do not give me one right at this moment I am getting up, leaving this office, never coming back and terminating therapy.

Doctor . . . I am counting to three. One . . . Two . . . Good-bye, Doctor.

After the monologue has been written it is time to act it. The only thing to make note of when acting an original monologue that is going to be used for a song is to remember that eventually the text of the monologue is going to disappear and you will be left only with the emotional and physical life of the monologue. Because of this you are not only allowed but *encouraged* to "indicate" while you are acting the lines of the monologue. In other words, you can actually act out exactly what you are talking about. Do not subtextualize the monologue, whatever you do. It is the subtext for the song, and we do not want to wind up with a subtext of a subtext.

The next step is to mesh the lyrics of the song with the monologue. We do this by inserting one line, thought, or idea from the lyric after one, two, or three lines of the monologue. It's sort of like doing a puzzle: We have so many lines of dialogue and so many lines of lyric. They are not even. They may not even always scan. When inserting, start at the top and work forward for a few lines. Then go to the end of the monologue and work backward for a few lines. Eventually you should meet somewhere near the middle where patches are less likely to show.

Here is how some of the insertions might look.

> *Dr. Korngold! . . . Thanks so much for seeing me on such short notice.*
> **Sometimes I feel such a desolation**
> *I don't know what I would have done if I couldn't have gotten an appointment.*
> **Words cannot convey . . .**
> *Things have been really lousy the past couple of days!*
> **The quiet, lonely desperation . . .**
> *It's the compulsive eating. . . . It's gotten considerably worse. (Wringing her hands.)*
> **That never goes away.**
> *I just can't stop the binging. (Shaking her head.)*
> **I'm like a playground no one plays in;**
> *I've never been out of control like this.*
> **A haunted house that no one stays in;**
> *(Looking frightened.)*

When did it start? ... Last week, ... right after my
graduation from "Smokequitters."
A vacant church that no one prays in ...
Yes, I know there is a connection, Dr. Korngold.
Empty and unused.
But knowing there is a connection and ending the con-
nection are two very different things!
Is it any wonder I'm confused.
Doctor! ... Is it really necessary for you to smoke during
our session?
I need someone in my life
Yes, I know you enjoy smoking, and that you don't have
the problem ...
When those empty feelings stab at me
but, ... (Hesitating.) ... Jesus H. Christ!
I need someone to inhabit me.
Right now I could kill for a cigarette.
Someone in my life.
Why? ... well, it's either that, or a cheese danish,
I need someone in the void
and the cheese danish is fattening, and not very practi-
cal right now.
Of my sleeping and my waking hours
Damn it! ... I'm addicted to nicotine. Isn't that reason
enough?
Who can end the angry aching hours.
I mean the food makes the pain go away, and the
cigarette helps me to forget I ever had the pain to begin
with.
Someone in my life.
No Doctor, ... I don't wnat to trace it back to early
childhood.
Someone in my world
I don't think it's important.
For my world's begun to reek of night.

It's my session, and I absolutely don't want to go back into that garbage. All I want is a cigarette.

Someone . . . who'll be the sun,

So please let me have one.

Not just a satellite.

My God! You can't mean that you're not going to let me have one!

There's a famine in my life.

I'm desperate. (Getting more and more upset.)

I need someone who can end this drought,

I'm not going to play by your rules. This is grossly unfair.

Bring the gentle rain I've done without

Here I am having a nicotine fit, and you're trying to tell me it's for my own good.

So I can see the grain grow,

(Suddenly quiet.) Doctor, I want a cigarette. I need a cigarette,

So I can be a rainbow.

. . . and if you do not give me one right at this moment

Someone to make me whole;

I am getting up, leaving this office, never coming back and terminating therapy.

To occupy my soul.

Doctor. . . . I am counting to three.

Someone!

One! . . .

Anyone!

Two! . . .

Someone!

Good-bye, Doctor.

Someone in my life.

Once the monologue and the insertions have been committed to memory, it is time to act out the monologue. When you get to the end of that part of the monologue where the lyric is inserted, you have to "freeze" and just say the lyric without acting it. The monologue already has provided you with the subtext that is to be acted. Remember that eventually the verbal life of the monologue is going to disappear. You will be left with its physical and emotional, or I should say dramatic, life. If you act the lyric at this point you will wind up filling the empty spaces with more than one acting beat, one based on the monologue and the other based on the lyric.

Also, in acting the monologue, don't be afraid to indicate and actually play the lines you are speaking. Again, remember that the monologue is going to eventually vanish, so it will not look like an obviously indicated performance when the physical life of the monologue becomes transposed to work with the lyric. Above all else, don't write a monologue that sounds like it is a letter being read. It must be a dramatic creation that causes physical and emotional responses that are visible on the actor. A cerebral monologue is as good as no monologue. Make it alive and vibrant.

I think that dramatic counterpoint really comes into its own when used with a flowery lyric that is highly stylized. The next example proves this point—it is my all-time favorite Rodgers and Hammerstein song, "You Are Never Away," from *Allegro*.

You Are Never Away

You are never away from your home in my heart;
There is never a day when you don't play a part
In a word that I say or a sight that I see
You are never away and I'll never be free.

You're the smile on my face, or a song that I sing!
You're a rainbow I chase on a morning in spring;
You're a star in the lace of a wild, willow tree—
In the green, leafy lace of a wild willow tree.

But tonight you're no star, nor a song that I sing;
In my arms, where you are, you are sweeter than
    spring;
In my arms, where you are, clinging closely to
    me,
You are lovelier by far than I dreamed you could
    be—
You are lovelier, my darling, than I dreamed you
    could be!

The song is a romantic up-tempo number that soars lyrically and musically. The reason this absolutely gorgeous song isn't used more frequently is that the lyric is not in today's vernacular. Most of us do not talk with the flowery passion with which Hammerstein endowed this lyric. To make this song work, most actors need to create a monologue that captures the passion but simplifies the content.

Upon analysis, the lyric reveals to us a young man impetuously and hopelessly head over heels in love with a beloved who is everything he could ever want. As a matter of fact, it is almost impossible to imagine his acting partner ever getting a word in edgewise, because he is so prolific in his praise of her.

Most actor/singers would find playing such an emotionally revealing song a difficult experience at an audition. Most would feel extremely vulnerable getting so physically and romantically worked up in front of strangers. The first step in defusing some of this vulnerability is to create a monologue that captures the passion and essence of the song but changes the acting partner and the dramatic situation.

Why not make the acting partner a man, a famous man. One the actor idolizes; one he is in awe of. Let's choose someone who would cause him to blurt out his feelings of admiration. For our purpose I have chosen Laurence Olivier. You would probably hear something like the following coming from almost any actor waiting on tables in this enviable circumstance.

"Oh my God! I don't believe this is really happening. Me serving dinner to Lord Laurence Olivier. You're my idol. I've seen almost everything you've ever done. This is the greatest moment of my entire life! Did you know I saw your Hamlet three times, your Richard the Third four times, and your Henry the Fifth six times. I even saw you play Becket on Broadway twice—first when you played Becket, and the second time when you reversed roles and played the king.

"Do you know what fascinates me most about you? You're an actor who is external and works inward. I mean, you care so much about the outward characteristics of whoever you are playing.

"For example, I loved your performance in *The Boys from Brazil*, when you played that famous Nazi hunter from Vienna who tracks down Dr. Mengele. But it wasn't until three months later that I saw a documentary on the actual Nazi hunter, Simon Weisenthal, that I realized he was the spitting image of your character. He not only looked like you, he talked like you did in the movie. It was then that I realized the full extent of your genius. Mr. Olivier, Lord Olivier . . . could I please have your autograph? Here's a pen. Oh, thank you so much. You've made my day!"

When we combine the monologue with the song we get the following interaction.

> *Oh my God! I don't believe this is really happening.*
> **You are never away from your home in my heart;**
> *Me serving dinner to Lord Laurence Olivier.*
> **There is never a day when you don't play a part**
> *You're my idol.*
> **In a word that I say**
> *I've seen almost everything you've ever done.*
> **Or a sight that I see**
> *This is the greatest honor of my entire life!*
> **You are never away and I'll never be free.**

I saw your Hamlet three times,
You're the smile on my face,
Your Richard the Third four times,
Or a song that I sing!
and your Henry the Fifth six times.
You're a rainbow I chase on a morning in spring;
I even saw you play Becket on Broadway twice.
You're a star in the lace of a wild, willow tree—
First when you played Becket,
In the green, leafy lace
and the second time when you reversed roles and played the king.
Of a wild willow tree.
Do you know what fascinates me most about you?
But tonight you're no star,
You're an actor who is external and works inward. I mean, you care so much about the outward characteristics of whoever you are playing.
Nor a song that I sing;
For example, I loved your performance in The Boys from Brazil *when you played that famous Nazi hunter from Vienna who tracks down Dr. Mengele.*
In my arms, where you are, you are sweeter than spring;
But it wasn't until three months later that I saw a documentary on the actual Nazi hunter, Simon Weisenthal, that I realized he was the spitting image of your character.
In my arms, where you are,
He not only looked like you, he talked like you did in the movie.
Clinging closely to me,
It was then that I realized the full extent of your genius.
You are lovelier by far than I dreamed you could be—

Mr. Olivier, Lord Olivier . . . could I please have your
autograph? Here's a pen.
You are lovelier, my darling, than I dreamed
Oh, thank you so much. You've made my day!
You could be!

One of the greatest things about using dramatic counterpoint and creating a monologue is that it forces the actor to *act* at an audition. When his or her concentration is on the monologue there is no time for self-evaluation and the stage fright that usually accompanies it.

As I have already mentioned, at a musical audition the actor/singer is better off singing a song that allows him to play himself, rather than sing a song that associates him with a particular character or character type. After all, at most auditions you have no way of knowing what parts have been cast and what roles are still available, or even what they are looking for. Sticking to the dictum of "be yourself," and carrying it even one step further, to "*play* yourself," is good solid advice I would most definitely follow.

There are two instances, however, when I would take exactly the opposite tack:

- When you know in advance exactly what character you are up for, such as when you are auditioning to replace someone who is leaving the cast, or auditioning for the national company, or bus and truck, of an existing musical.

- When you are auditioning for a new musical, never produced before, which is based on an existing novel, play, or film, and you have been asked to audition for the specific role of a well-known character.

In both these instances, playing yourself will not help you to be considered for the part nearly as much as trying to zero in on playing the character they are looking for. To achieve this, use subtext once again.

Wouldn't it be simpler just to learn a song that is already sung by that particular character? No! It takes several weeks of living with a piece of material before it truly becomes part of you. If you try to audition with it before that, you will be concentrating so much on making sure the lyrics are correct, the music is perfect, and the characterization so on-target that you will never be relaxed enough to pull it off. At most you will give a second-hand imitation of what your audience has already seen performed by the character's original creator, staged and mounted, costumed, and accompanied to their satisfaction. There is no way you can compete with that.

The only sure way of proving to them that you are right for the part is to use one of the existing numbers from your repertoire and subtextualize it so you are playing it as a statement the character might make.

How do you accomplish this? By using the monologue technique and creating an imaginary situation that the character you will be playing could feasibly be involved in. Here are two examples.

Some years ago I was coaching a young actor called Steve, who had done lots of TV and films but had never sung before, at least not in a musical. We had been working for only a few weeks, and he had only one song under his belt, a rather beautiful ballad by Cy Coleman and Dorothy Fields from the movie version of *Sweet Charity*. Shirley Maclaine sang it to John McMartin, who had passed out in an elevator in which they were both trapped between floors. The two of them had just met when the elevator jammed, and he went out cold.

Here is the lyric, with appropriate changes to allow its being sung by a man.

It's a Nice Face

It's a nice face!
As faces go, it's a very nice face.
With a place for every feature,

Every feature in its place.
Not a commonplace face.

Her eyes? Clear.
Her chin? Stubborn, but strong.
Her ears? They're ordinary ears.
Her nose? A trifle long.

Still, it's a gentle face.
A little square, a little corny,
It's a sentimental face.

Here's a girl I've only met.
Here's a girl I should forget, yet!

I won't make this a federal case.
It's just another pretty face,
But, it's a very, very, very nice face.

The song was right for Steve because it is a beautifully crafted work that does not require a legitimate large baritone voice since it is conversational in nature. It is easy to sing because the tessitura (vocal range) is not too extensive. Also, the song does not require long sustained notes from the actor, and therefore does not reveal vocal weaknesses. It was also the right song for an actor to choose because it is filled with the dramatic conflict of a man who is in the process of realizing that he is smitten with someone he's just met.

No sooner had Steve learned the number, and we had it staged, when his agent called him. He had set up an audition for Steve to sing for Harold Prince and Stephen Sondheim, who were casting for their forthcoming Broadway musical, *A Little Night Music.*

Steve was understandably upset. He was being submitted for the part of Count Carl-Magnus, a conceited, egocentric, militaristic officer and gentleman. A man who believed the whole world revolved around him, and that he existed by Divine Right. A character quite similar to that of Miles Gloriosus in *A Funny Thing Happened on the Way to the Forum.*

Steve not only was nothing like the character he was up for, but he had nothing in his repertoire that was suitable, and we had no time to find and learn something fitting. Since the show was as yet unproduced we had nothing to go by except the character description in the script.

We decided that there was no reason not to sing "It's a Nice Face," but that it should be performed as if it were written for Count Carl-Magnus. How would he feel and act if he found himself gripped by an obsession with a woman who was his inferior. Wouldn't he feel disgust, anger (to the point of fury), and a great deal of contempt? Here is how Steve subtextualized the number, playing Count Magnus:

> *(After a flirtation with a serving girl, one obviously quite beneath his exalted station:)*
> *I bet she'd be good for a roll in the hay.*
> **It's a nice face.**
> *After all she's not bad-looking.*
> **As faces go, it's a very nice face.**
> *She's clean,*
> **With a place for every feature,**
> *She kind of smells nice,*
> **Every feature in its place,**
> *I bet she'd really be fun for a roll in the hay.*
> **Not a commonplace face.**
> *(Scratching his chin, rather puzzled by this fascination.)*
> *Just what about her is turning me on?*
> **Her eyes?**
> *Does she remind me of somebody?*
> **Clear.**
> *I wonder whom.*
> **Her chin? Stubborn,**

Just what the hell is so fascinating about her?
But strong.
Is it the way she moves?
Her ears?
(Gleefully) I really like the way she moves!
They're ordinary ears.
I wonder if she can keep her mouth shut.
Her nose?
(Shaking his head.) She'd probably blab to the rest of the servants.
A trifle long.
Still, I think she'd be worth taking the risk.
Still,
(Softening a little.) I haven't wanted anyone this badly in a long time.
It's a gentle face.
It might really be wonderful.
A little square, a little corny.
Think how lucky she'd be to be with glorious me.
It's a sentimental face.
Christ! What the hell is getting into me!
Here's a girl I've only met.
I must have gone through a temporary obsession.
Here's a girl I should forget, yet!
(Magnus stalks around, the tension building.) I must get hold of myself.
I won't make this a federal case,
I must definitely see my doctor in the morning.
It's just another pretty face,
Besides, she might have been with . . . anybody!
But it's a very, very, very nice
(With painful resignation.) Damn it, I want her.
Face.

Steve was amazed to be called back not once, not twice, but more than four times. They asked him to sing, then read, then sing again, then read again. It was between Steve and Laurence Guitard, and Guitard finally got it. Vocally and dramatically he was more on target.

So why did Steve get so many callbacks? Because every time he sang "It's a Nice Face," a song totally wrong for the character they were looking for, the character they were trying to cast kept hitting them right between the eyes. They didn't know that what they were seeing was a skilled actor's subtext. They thought Steve was really like that, and it was for real.

The second story I'd like to tell you involves another one of my students, Filis, a lovely soprano who was going to a chorus call for replacements for the national company of *Nine*. Although she was told they would only hear sixteen bars of a song (see Chapter 7), we decided she would start from the top. She had a decent-sized repertoire, but there was nothing in it that was right for the part of Guido's wife. We decided to use an existing song in her repertoire, "Here in My Arms," by Rodgers & Hart.

"Here in My Arms" is a rather beautiful ingenue soprano ballad. The lyric deals with being too shy to admit to one's true feelings of loving someone, and being unable to tell them.

Here in My Arms

(verse)
I know a pretty place at your command, sir;
It's not a city place, yet near at hand, sir;
Here, if you loll away, two hearts can toll away.
You'd never stroll away, if you only knew!

(chorus)
Here in my arms it's adorable!
It's deplorable that you were never there.
When little lips are so kissable

It's permissable for me to ask my share.
Next to my heart it is ever so lonely,
I'm holding only air,
While here in my arms it's adorable!
It's deplorable that you were never there.

At first glance, the song was totally wrong for the wife in
Nine. After all, she leaves him after a confrontation in which
she decides she will no longer put up with all his infidelities
year after year. She is no ingenue and she is certainly no longer
shy about what she feels. Filis decided to subtextualize the lyric
by creating the reconciliation scene in which the wife decides to
forgive Guido and tells him what she went through during
their separation. Her subtext went something like this:

(With great personal resolution and strength.) Guido,
I've got something important to tell you.
I know a pretty place at your command, Sir.
This is not going to be easy.
It's not a city place, yet near at hand, Sir;
I'm coming back to you, (beat)
Here if you loll away
. . . but only on my terms.
Two hearts can toll away
I've put up with a lot of indignities the past years . . .
You'd never stroll away
Haven't you been aware of the pain you've caused me?
If you only knew!
Like your forgetting my birthday,
Here in my arms it's adorable
our anniversary,
It's deplorable that you were never there.
but your infidelities, which I pretended did not exist, at
least for the rest of the world,
When little lips are so kissable

They were just too much.
It's permissable for me to ask my share.
Did you know I thought of divorcing you?
Next to my heart it is ever so lonely,
I was very angry and confused.
I'm holding only air,
But we do have a son to think of.
Here in my arms
Guido, I know you love me and need me.
It's adorable!
I've always loved you and the fact that you need me is what had made me decide to stay.
It's deplorable
Thank God! You've come to your senses and confessed everything to me.
That you were never
We can have a wonderful life. Our son can have brothers and sisters.
There!

It worked like magic. They didn't stop her after sixteen bars. She not only sang the full chorus, but sang two additional songs as well and was asked to read and come back. Had *Nine* not closed, and had the producers not used the original cast for the national company, there is every likelihood that Filis would be touring with it right now.

The important fact I want to convey to you is that you don't need an extensive repertoire of songs in your audition trunk, just as you don't require an extensive, expensive wardrobe of clothes in your closet. A few good songs chosen intelligently can lend themselves admirably to doing double or even triple duty if necessary, just by the judicious use of subtext and acting techniques. Anybody in the business should have the knowledge and capability to create a subtext that gives new and varied life to the songs that he or she uses already. The important thing is to know when to be yourself, and when not to be yourself.

CHAPTER

3

What To Sing and How To Sing It

Acting a song requires a thorough knowledge of acting techniques, including not only the use of subtext, but the ability to convince one's audience that an acting partner is there when in reality there is no one there. Singing a song, on the other hand, requires not only considerable acting skills but vocal skills, a great deal of intelligence, and a lot of sensitivity as well.

If we are to act and sing songs, it stands to reason that we have to know a little bit about them. Songs are made up of several components: the lyric, the music, and the accompaniment. A song can serve specific functions. It can serve as "background" where it doesn't have to stand up to close scrutiny and is almost subliminal in its effect. A song can be a solo, a duet, a trio, or a chorus piece involving an entire ensemble. It can be in a foreign language or it can be a translation into English. It can be a Negro spiritual or a piece designed to be sung in a cathedral. It can be a folk song that has been handed down for generations or it can be the latest rock hit hot off the presses. *Or* it can be a piece that was conceived to work theatrically, that is, designed for the stage or for a musical film. This is the material that the actor will be concerned with.

Popular songs, at least those that were created to sell a lot of records, owe their life to the electronic channeling, reverberation, amplification, and balancing that takes place in the recording studio. Through equalization, the volume, more or less, stays constant. Because of all the electronic gimmickry one is readily hypnotized by the beat, arrangement, instrumentation, and vocal delivery. With few exceptions, the lyric is simplistic, to say the least. Most contemporary popular songs are designed to a specific formula that registers as being "catchy" on first hearing. I once heard a songwriter who was addressing a group explain, "When you first hear it, it should sound like you've already heard it fifty times but want to hear it another couple of hundred times more." This helps us understand the life span of most pop songs. They tend to be on the charts for a certain limited period of time, after which they quickly fade to obscurity.

Pop songs never work as audition songs for the simple reason that because they were designed to be sung into a microphone they don't project past the radius of a few feet. There is no acting partner implied most of the time, and they just don't have enough "meat" in the lyric to sustain any dramatic interest. Since the instrumental feeling is so important to the entire structure, the vocalist tries to blend in with the instrumental ensemble. In doing so he or she becomes for the most part unintelligible.

Years ago pop music was written by the same giant talents who contributed so richly to the musical theatre. Julie Styne, Frank Loesser, Rodgers and Hammerstein, Irving Berlin, Burton Lane, Alan Jay Lerner, Johnny Mercer, Jerome Kern, and scores of others were the biggies of the pop scene. The songs from numerous Broadway musicals became staples of the popular song market. All that changed in the mid-fifties with the appearance of Elvis Presley, and later, the Beatles. Suddenly the staples that everyone was used to became passé and the music of the theatre was for the first time in history no longer the popular music of the masses.

It is theatrical music that we are really interested in. Since the lyric is a script that has to be acted, we want material that provides the best dramatic script that's around.

What's so special about a show tune? Well, for one thing, if the moment it was meant to highlight and capture in a show wasn't so important dramatically it wouldn't have been written in the first place. It has built-in "actability." There is almost always a specific acting partner implied. But there are show tunes and there are show tunes. Some of them work admirably as audition material. Others unfortunately don't fare as well, since they were written to fulfill other specific purposes. Let's see if we can't zero in on some practical guidelines to use in selecting the right songs to suit our particular needs. Here are the types of numbers found in a typical musical; and let's see what *won't* work.

The Wrong Kinds of Audition Songs

SONG-AND-DANCE NUMBERS

These were written and conceived to be danced as solos, something you don't usually do at a vocal audition. If at your audition the choreographer has any questions as to your ability to move or dance, he or she will usually have you dance at a separate dance audition.

It's funny to see dancing combined with a song at an audition. Don't try it unless you are a dancer/singer auditioning for a revival of a show like *Gypsy,* and you are up for the part of Tulsa and have to sing "All I Need Now Is the Girl."

Examples of song-and-dance numbers are: "Put on a Happy Face" from *Bye Bye Birdie,* "Once in Love with Amy" from *Where's Charlie,* and "The Music and the Mirror" from *A Chorus Line.* The danger of singing a song-and-dance number is that the lyrics have been written to be very simple so that they will not upstage the dancing and so that the dancing will not obscure the lyric. These lyrics do not serve the actor well as a script to act at an audition. They were meant to be danced to, not acted.

PRODUCTION NUMBERS

These are similar to dance numbers except that instead of dancing there are production values going on that are essential to the lifeblood of the song. There might be all kinds of scenery flying in and out as the number is being sung. Or there might be lighting changes, crowds of people rushing around, or some kind of comic business. Certainly none of this could happen at a solo audition, and these missing production values make any performer look limited if he or she sings a production number out of the context of a show.

Examples of production numbers are: "I'm Gonna Wash That Man Right Out of My Hair" from *South Pacific*, during which Nellie Forbush is shampooing her hair and being razzed by the other Army nurses—the song is wonderful on stage within the context of the show but a bore when sung by an actress just standing in place at an audition; "You've Gotta Have Heart" from *Damn Yankees*, sung by a baseball coach to his team in a locker room, trying to inspire them to regain their winning streak—at an audition, where's the team? Where's the excitement?; and "You Gotta Have a Gimmick" from *Gypsy*, sung by three strippers in full regalia and props including a trumpet, outrageous costumes, and a set of electric lights—this would hardly work as a solo number.

SIGNATURE SONGS

These are songs that are too closely identified with the famous performers who "created" them. The danger of singing these songs at auditions is that the memory of the originator will overshadow you and prevent the auditors from seeing you objectively. Examples of signature songs are "Over the Rainbow," forever the property of Judy Garland; "If Ever I Would Leave You," which will probably always be identified with Robert Goulet; and "Maybe This Time," the signature tune of Liza Minelli.

FICTIONAL CHARACTER SONGS

These numbers are so firmly identified with certain fictional characters that your audience will automatically assume that you can only play that type of part. The only time you should sing them is if you are up for one of these roles in a revival of the show. Examples of fictional character songs are "Soliloquy" from *Carousel*, where the actor is playing Billy Bigelow; "Hello, Young Lovers" from *The King and I*, where the actress is playing Anna; and "If I Were a Rich Man" from *Fiddler on the Roof*, where it is almost impossible for the performer not to be representing himself as a would-be Tevye. Some other examples would have to include "Little Girls" from *Annie* (Miss Hannigan), "I Can't Say No" from *Oklahoma* (Ado Annie), and "Don't Rain on My Parade" from *Funny Girl* (this last song is doubly lethal because it is not only identified with the character of Fanny Brice but is a Barbra Streisand signature song as well).

Remember, the people you are auditioning for know every standard show in the repertoire inside out. They associate songs with characters the way we associate accents and dialects with geographical locations.

PLOTLINE NUMBERS

These were written to do only one thing, help to further the plot of a musical. They do little to help the actor establish who he or she really is as a person. These could also be called narrative songs because, while singing them, the actor is busy playing storyteller. They rob actors of their own lives. How often do we really look at storytellers? Examples of these numbers are "The King's New Clothes" by Frank Loesser from the movie *Hans Christian Andersen;* "Sensitivity" from *Once Upon a Mattress*; and "You Did It" from *My Fair Lady*.

VOGUE NUMBERS

These are numbers from shows that are currently playing, which are to be avoided because everybody is singing them;

they are overexposed. Besides that, there is no way you can compete with the performance that the people auditing you have, most likely, recently seen on stage. The memory of the original performance with lights, costume, blocking, and staging accompanied by full orchestra is something you cannot hope to equal or even compete with in an audition situation. The only time I would venture a performance of one of these songs at a musical audition is if the song was specifically requested, and you are being considered as a replacement for one of the parts in that particular show.

Now that we have discussed what not to sing, let's find material that we *can* sing, material that will work for us at a musical audition.

In-One Numbers

One type of musical number that we haven't discussed at all is the in-one number. These songs are the best choice for audition material. In-one numbers are hardly being written anymore for musicals. Before I tell you why they're so perfect for auditions, let's see how they evolved and why they're not being written today.

In one is the term that defines the playing area of the stage that exists between the proscenium curtain and the footlights, or orchestra pit. In the 1960s great innovations were taking place in the realm of theatrical set design. Parts of the set could now "fly" in, while other pieces could roll in, and still others slide and glide in. Set design has now become so sophisticated that it is unnecessary for most shows even to use the proscenium curtain. These innovations have given a continuity to the musical theatre that approaches that of film, in that the transition from scene to scene does not have to be interrupted. But there is always a price to pay for such new techniques, and the price has been high. This particular innovation killed the need to write beautiful ballads and other numbers to cover scene changes.

In the olden days (pre-sixties) when a change of scene was necessary, all the stagehands would change the set behind a traveler (curtain) that would close and hide the scene change. Composers and lyricists would write beautiful songs to be sung while the scene change was going on. The verse to these songs, if they had one, was sung in the existing set. At the end of the verse the performer would cheat (move) downstage in front of the traveler, which would close behind him or her. The chorus, or main part of the song, would be sung all the way downstage, as close to the orchestra as one could get. At the end of the song the curtain would open and the next scene would begin.

Obviously, the in-one number had great advantages for the actor who was singing it. As he cheated downstage from the verse to the chorus he became more important to the audience the closer he got to them. When the traveler closed behind him he was no longer competing with a set or with anyone or anything else on stage. These numbers stopped the show even if they were ballads. Some examples of in-one numbers are "On the Street Where You Live" from *My Fair Lady*, "If He Walked Into My Life" from *Mame*, and "Losing My Mind" from *Follies*.

What makes in-one numbers so ideal for audition purposes is that the audition situation is physically very similar to the original dramatic or theatrical circumstances of the song. In both you have one actor alone onstage. No set or scenery. Simple lighting, and an accompaniment. The only major differences are that in the show you would be in costume with a follow spot or pinspot on you, and you would have an orchestral accompaniment. But these differences are slight and the effect of the number would be about the same. One loses nothing in the transition from stage to rehearsal studio.

How do you find them? How do you recognize them? Most of them have become standards. "Someone to Watch Over Me," "The Man I Love," "Little Girl Blue," "My Funny Valentine," "I Got Lost in His Arms," "The Party's Over," "I've Grown Accustomed to Her Face". . . . They're all in-one numbers.

Remember when I said that the pop writers of yesterday

where the writers of Broadway musicals from the same era? Look through a Jerome Kern songbook, or a Rodgers and Hart or Rodgers and Hammerstein songbook. Look at all the theatre collections at your music store. They're all there. Look into the published collections of Irving Berlin, Cole Porter, Lerner and Loewe, Burton Lane, Julie Styne, Harold Arlen, and George and Ira Gershwin. These are just the tip of the iceberg. If you have access to a library that has an extensive collection of recordings of Broadway musicals, start listening and you'll find what you are looking for.

To help you along, I have provided toward the end of the book a list of more than 130 songs that are good examples of repertoire suitable for auditioning and performing—in-one numbers, all of them. This list is by no means exhaustive or complete, and reflects only my tastes in material. You will find many of your favorites missing, not because I don't love them— I'm sure I do—but because the purpose of this list is to give you a source of underexposed material. You will find these songs in Chapter 13.

What makes these songs so unique? Quality! They were written by masters who made melodies flow the way TV sitcoms gurgle forth in our era. They are marked by a quality of lyric not to be found in popular or show music today, with few exceptions. The most important consideration for the singer is the lyric and what to do with it.

Making the Lyric Come Alive

From the moment singers start to sing a song the lyric becomes their property. They then have the obligation to play lyricist, and make the lyric come alive as if they had indeed created it. What marks the difference between a singer and an artist is the interpretation of a lyric. The voice performs only half of the song, and remains only an instrument until words galvanize it and focus it into a completely new and fulfilling entity.

But how does one make a lyric come alive? Well, there are several good ways, and they are so obvious that you will probably kick yourself for not having discovered them sooner. Here are a few of them.

ESSENTIAL AND NONESSENTIAL WORDS

If you were to analyze our spoken language the way we are used to hearing it spoken, it would readily become apparent that not everything we say is given equal emphasis. Let me illustrate this by quoting the Pledge of Allegiance. The accented words I will capitalize and the unaccented words will be in lower case letters. "i PLEDGE ALLEGIANCE to the FLAG of the UNITED STATES of AMERICA, and to the REPUBLIC for WHICH it STANDS, ONE NATION INDIVISIBLE under GOD with LIBERTY and JUSTICE for ALL."

In the above example there were fifteen unessential words and fourteen essential words, nearly an even match. Why is this important? Because most singers and actors, when they sing, waste their time singing into and stressing words that do not require emphasis in the first place. This causes them to tire quickly. Many become convinced they can't sing successfully and some give up unnecessarily. Singing words that *should* be stressed helps language to flow the way we are used to hearing it and helps the actor/singer to give better line readings. An added bonus is that the words become more intelligible as well.

COLOR WORDS

These are the words that we automatically accent because they are descriptive. They are verbs, adjectives, and adverbs. Here are some ordinary, everyday sentences that one might encounter in third grade. Notice what gets accented and why?

What a beautiful girl! (adjective)
You're driving me crazy! (verb)

That was wonderfully and skillfully acted! (two adverbs followed by the verb)

When we highlight these words while we are singing, we add a depth and aliveness to our performance that makes it a "first-time" experience for our audience. It is almost as if we had written the text ourselves and were quite proud of it. Caressing the color words by singing into them creates much better line readings. If you are auditioning for an original musical, and the lyricist is there and you can impress him with the fact that you will do justice to his lyrics, you stand a much better chance of landing that role than your competition.

LIQUID CONSONANTS

These are consonants on which one can produce musical sounds. In other words, you can sing *on* the consonant itself. Liquid consonants are the Ls, Ms, and Ns. Voice teachers sometimes vocalize their students on La La La, Ma Ma Ma, or Na Na Na for this reason. When singing accented words like the color words (verbs, adjectives, and adverbs), if they start on a liquid consonant think of them as two-syllable words. For example: I LL-Love you. You are NN-Never away. You're just too MM-Marvelous. Believe it or not, if you sing them this way you will be amazed by the richness of sound that comes out and by the size of the voice you never knew you had if you're a nonsinger. If you are a singer you'll be surprised by the richness in tone liquids can give you.

PLOSIVES

Plosives are consonants produced by the lips and are sometimes called lip consonants. Most of us when we were children had the experience of blowing out a candle by saying the letter "P" from several feet away. The other lip consonants are B, F, and V. In addition to P, hard Ts, Ks, and Ds are also like plosives. Try putting your hand in front of your mouth and saying them forcefully. You should feel a slight explosion of air. It is the force of this explosion, when coupled with the vowel sound that immediately follows it, that projects the word with a greater intensity and larger sound than the vowel is capable of producing alone.

Think of the consonant as similar to the valve on a water fountain. When you press down the valve on the fountain the water may initially leap up to a height of five or six inches. Right after that spurt the height of the column will drop to one or two inches—barely high enough for us to press our lips to the fountain without touching it. What has happened is that the normal water pressure, which is the equivalent of the vowel, is only sufficient to raise the water to the height of one or two inches. The sudden release by pressing down on the valve forcefully releases built-up pressure and is equivalent to attaching the consonant, especially the plosive, to the vowel. It gives the vowel a more forceful, robust sound than could have been gotten from just singing "on" the vowel itself.

ALLITERATION

Alliteration is a poetic device in which several words that start with the same consonant or sound are used together. "Lovely ladies like to listen to lush lyrics." More commonly in lyrics you will find lines such as "me and my shadow," "time after time," "hard-hearted Hannah," and other similar lines. When you sing them, caress the consonants and sing into them so they stand out. It will make the lyric come to life.

ONOMATOPOEIA

This is another poetic device, this time employing words that sound like what they are describing. Words like tinkle, crash, boom, plop, and frigid are onomatopoeiac. In songs such as Hugh Martin and Ralph Blaine's "The Trolley Song" onomatopoeia abounds. Be sure when you sing it or others like it you highlight words like *clang, clang, clang* or *chug, chug, chug*.

PHRASING

Phrasing is the most misunderstood craft there is. Actors and singers who would never dream of speaking in run-on sentences feel little guilt in singing that way when they massacre a song. They seem to have been taught by their voice teachers that singing an unbroken musical line shows great musicianship. All it shows is breath control, which might be necessary in oratorio, lieder, or opera. Such singing is never called for in a musical. It is more important that the dramatic script, in this case the lyric, comes alive, sounding and feeling as if this were the first and only time these words will ever be said.

When we speak, we say a few words, pause, say a few more, and finish our sentence. If you notice, there are four pauses in the previous sentence. The actor or singer is obligated to separate *all* words that could have a slight pause between them by using a glottal stop, which is no more than a vocal comma. (One closes the glottis in the throat.) If the performer neglects to do this simple thing, he sounds like someone who is tired of doing the song. The words are utterly predictable, have no surprises, are lifeless, drab, and dull, and will not be taken seriously by those forced to listen.

The Anatomy of a Song

In writing this chapter I went through every dictionary I could get my hands on; none of the definitions I found really tell what a song is. First of all I think we can agree that a song is a brief musical composition written for voice. The voice obviously is singing something, usually words or text of some kind. What makes the song distinct from recitative (sung text delivered in the rhythm of speech) is that there is a basic poetic form and rhyme scheme to it.

In classical songs, also known as "art" songs or lieder, there are no restrictions as to length or accompaniment. Certainly the songs of Mahler and Richard Strauss bear this out. They have huge orchestral accompaniments for full symphony orchestras, and they are not brief. Some of them may last for fifteen minutes. The songs of Brahms, Schubert, Schumann, and Fauré are much shorter and were written with piano accompaniment.

I have already discussed the popular song and how it evolved in this country, so I needn't go on about its history. Instead let's discuss briefly the different forms it may take, and the different parts it may contain.

The standard pop song known today, and has been known for the past hundred years or so, usually has thirty-two bars to it. (A bar of music is the same thing as a measure, and the two terms are used interchangeably.) These thirty-two bars divide themselves into four groups of eight measures, called the first eight, the second eight, the third eight, and the fourth or final eight. The entire thirty-two measures that make up the song are referred to as the *chorus*. In older songs these thirty-two measures are sometimes called the *refrain*, or even *burthen*. (Jerome Kern used that expression on almost all of his songs.) These terms are interchangeable and mean exactly the same thing.

Sometimes there is an additional piece of music and lyrics that may occur before the chorus, which is called the *verse* to the song. The only relationship it has to the song musically is that the verse and the song may be in the same key or tonality. Lyrically, however, the relationship is much more powerful and potent. Let's examine a typical verse to a song and see what it does, and why it is so crucial.

> When Louie came home to the flat
> He hung up his coat and his hat.
> He gazed all around but no wifey he found,
> So he said, "Where can Flossie be at?"
> A note on the table, he spied.
> He read it just once, and he cried.
> It read, "Louie dear, it's too slow for me here
> So, I think I will go for a ride!"

This is the verse to one of best-known songs of a hit movie, a song that gave the movie its title and helped establish a young singer's stardom.

The reason why, to an actor, this verse is so crucial to the song is that it gives the actor and his audience the following bits of information:

1. Louie is married.

2. His wife's name is Flossie.

3. He expected her to be home.

4. He loves her.

5. She has left him, at least temporarily.

6. She left him because it was too "slow" for her. She's bored.

The contents of Flossie's note, which continues in the chorus of the song, will provide us with the rest of the information we need to know. Here it is now:

> "Meet me in St. Louis, Louie.
> Meet me at the fair.
> Don't tell me the lights are shining
> Any place but there.
> We will dance the hoochy koochy.
> I will be your tootsy wootsy,
> If you will meet me in St. Louis, Louie.
> Meet me at the fair."

The important thing to note about verses is that they give a whole new dimension to the meaning of the words in the

---

"Meet Me in St. Louis," lyrics and music by Kerry Mills and Andrew B. Stirling. Public domain.

chorus. They are not only expositional, as can be seen in the example opposite, but they *justify* the reason for singing the chorus. Most choruses seem to me a bit out of context when heard without the verse.

Should you sing the verse to a song if it has one? Most definitely, if you are an actor. The verse answers the questions of where, why, when, how, and who. It sets up the chorus and makes it more meaningful and believable to whoever may be auditioning you. The only times I would omit the verse are: if the audition is for a chorus part, and they do not have the time to hear an entire number; or if the verse, instead of setting up the song, hinders it because it contains too much information relating to the original plot of the musical the song is from. (Examples of this latter situation are "How Can I Wait Till Tomorrow Comes" from *Paint Your Wagon*, "I've Grown Accustomed to Her Face" from *My Fair Lady*, and "Hello, Young Lovers" from *The King and I*.)

A very embarrassing moment in my life happened when through youthful ignorance I allowed one of my students, whom I was accompanying at the audition, to sing the chorus of "I'm in Love, I'm in Love, with Miss Logan" from *New Faces of 1952* at the auditions of the Broadway show *All American*. I was still a graduate student at Juilliard and at that time I knew nothing of the importance of verses. I walked onstage, where the piano was, with my student, Peter. He began to sing. We had gotten no more than six or seven bars into the song when someone shouted, "Okay, who the hell put you up to this?" What neither of us had realized up until then was that Joshua Logan was the director of *All American*, and it must have appeared that we were purposely insulting the man by questioning his masculinity in our choice of song.

Had Peter sung the verse to the song it would have been absolutely clear that Josh Logan was not the acting partner, nor subject, of the song.

HOW TO SING A VERSE

Since the verse is expositional, and the information that it delivers is so crucial to setting up the chorus, the lyrics of the verse must be delivered quickly in a way that requires the least amount of concentration on the part of the audience. Most of the time this means that the verse will be sung in "the rhythm of speech," or *ad lib*, as it is usually called. I would like to emphasize that although the term ad lib may mean "very slow" to a jazz singer in a nightclub, in reality it means "at the liberty of the performer."

The great composers realized how important it was to allow the lyric of the verse to be easily heard when they set the verses of their lyricists to music. If you look at the verses of Rodgers and Hart songs, you will notice that they are so simply constructed that the melodies are quite often made up of only one, two, or three notes that are almost nursery rhyme–like in effect (for example, "It Never Entered My Mind," "I Could Write a Book," and "Ten Cents a Dance"). George Gershwin was a bit more melodic in composing the music for his verses, yet they are simple just the same. Other composers such as Vernon Duke and Harold Arlen wrote music for their verses that is almost atonal, or nonmelodic in its effect. The reasons are still the same—to make sure the verse is heard, that it doesn't upstage the chorus, and that it doesn't unnecessarily slow down its delivery.

SINGING THE CHORUS

Let's get back to the chorus of a song. We have already said that it usually contains thirty-two measures divided into four eight-measure sections. The song also has a form, and that can be of only two different kinds, or variations of these two kinds.

A song can either take the form of AABA or ABAB. Please don't think that this is going to get mathematical or technical. It isn't. The only reason you have to know the form of a song is so that you will known when and where to move within the song.

You see, between these eight-measure sections of the song there are large empty spaces that are called "air." It is in these spaces that you would walk or move during the performance to sustain visual interest in yourself. Let's take another look at the chorus of "Meet Me in St. Louis" so we can make this a little clearer.

> **Meet me in St. Louis, Louie.**
> **Meet me at the fair.**

This is the first A section and first eight measures of the chorus.

> **Don't tell me the lights are shining**
> **Any place but there.**

This is the second A section and the second eight measures of the chorus.

> **We will dance the hootchy kootchy**
> **You will be my tootsy wootsy if you will . . .**

This is the B section and the third eight measures of the chorus.

> **Meet me in St. Louis, Louie.**
> **Meet me at the fair.**

This is the third and final A section, and the last, or fourth, eight measures of the chorus.

In an AABA song the first A is eight measures long. It is then musically repeated with a different lyric, so we hear the same A section, possibly with a slight variation, that is again eight measures long. Next comes an eight-measure section of music that is musically different from what we have heard before and which "releases" us from the monotony of the two A sections. This B section is appropriately called the "release." It is followed again by a reprise of the A section, which again is eight measures in length.

The ABAB song differs only in that each A section is followed by a B section. This easily divides the song into two sections of AB. The second AB section usually is more developed and slightly more intricate than the first AB section, especially the B part.

Here is a perfect example of this form of song:

> **Take me out to the ballgame.**
> **Take me out to the crowd.**

This is the first eight measures. We call it A.

> **Buy me some peanuts and crackerjack.**
> **I don't care if we never get back, for it's ...**

This is the second eight measures, or B section. It isn't a release because it symmetrically balances the A.

> **Root, root, root for the home team.**
> **If they don't win it's a shame.**

Here in the third eight-measure section we have A again with a slight variation of melodic notes on "they don't win it's a shame." Since it is slightly different, let's call it A2.

> **For it's one! two! three strikes!, you're out!**
> **At the old ball game.**

Notice here, in the final eight-measure section, that this is a completely new melody. We have not heard it before. We could call it C, but that would be confusing. It symmetrically balances the A2 section that precedes it so we call it B2.

Other examples of ABAB songs are "Embracable You," "Moon River," "What I Did for Love," and Billy Joel's "Just the Way You Are."

All songs are either one or the other of these song forms we have just discussed, or some variation of them. In more contemporary numbers the song may be elongated by the addition of other sections, usually another A and B. Sometimes an "Interlude" section is added to contrast with the monotony of the repeated AABA or ABAB if there is more than one chorus to the song. In any event they are all variations or extensions of these same two standard song forms.

Here is an example of an extended AABA song that has an interlude followed by an additional A section. At the very end of the song is a small extension that is usually called a tag. The tag gives a sense of finality to the song so you know it is definitely over. What is remarkable about this song's construction is that the chorus has only twenty-four measures instead of the usual thirty-two. Perhaps the extreme slowness of the tempo of the chorus makes it almost imperceptible. I didn't discover that it was twenty-four measures until I referred to the music in order to copy the lyric down for you.

Ten Cents a Dance

(verse)
I work at the palace ballroom,
But, gee, that "palace" is cheap;
When I go home to my chilly hall room
I'm much too tired to sleep.

I'm one of those lady teachers,
A beautiful hostess, you know,
One that the palace features
At exactly a dime a throw.

(chorus)
Ten cents a dance; that's what they pay me.
Gosh, how they weigh me down!
(A section— 4 measures long)

Ten cents a dance, pansies and rough guys,
Tough guys who tear my gown!
(A2 section—4 measures long)

Seven to midnight, I hear drums,
Loudly the saxophone blows,
Trumpets are tearing my ear-drums.
Customers crush my toes.
(Release, the third eight, B)

Sometimes I think I've found my hero
But, it's a "queer" romance.
All that you need is a ticket,
Come on big boy, ten cents a dance.
(Final eight, A2)

(interlude)
Fighters and sailors and bow-legged tailors
Can pay for their tickets and rent me!
Butchers and barbers and rats from the harbors
Are sweet-hearts my good luck has sent me.

Though I've a chorus of elderly beaux,
Stockings are porous with holes at the toes.
I'm here till closing time,
Dance and be merry, it's only a dime.

(final eight)
Sometimes I think I've found my hero
But it's a queer romance,
All that you need is a ticket!
Come on big boy, ten cents a dance!

Keys and Transpositions

One of the most frequently misunderstood topics related to singing is the subject of keys and transpositions. Many singers have been led to believe that it is wrong to sing a song in any but the published key. They sometimes refer to the published key as the "original" key. Nothing could be farther from the truth.

The simple fact is that with very few exceptions there is no such thing as an original key. Even in "classical" music the songs of Schubert, Brahms, Fauré, Schumann, Mahler, Richard Strauss, and others are published in several keys for high, medium, or low voice. Songs are meant to be sung in any key that makes them sound good. The *only* exceptions are Grand Opera and symphonic lieder, where the keys are definitely set and are part of the orchestral texture of the whole work.

When keys are set, it is only because it is economically mandatory to do so. I am thinking, of course, of the Broadway musical. While a musical is in rehearsal there is no such thing as a "set" key. It is not until it is time for the orchestrations of the songs to be written that anyone starts thinking about what key the song should be written in. Once the keys have been set, for whoever happens to be singing those songs, they are frozen in those keys forever after. The reason is clear enough: it is easier to hire someone who can sing the songs in the keys in which the orchestrations are written than to reorchestrate, which would cost thousands of dollars per number. Of course, if you have the money, and the only thing standing between you and that part you want is the fact that the keys are too high or low, then offer to pay for reorchestrating your numbers. Producers are easily wooed by economic sensibility.

Therefore, if you are not singing a song from a show that you are auditioning for, then you can sing the song you are using *in any key that shows you off to best advantage*. One more thing: no one sings in a particular key. A key is particular only to a song, and one finds that key by seeing how the song lies in one's tessitura, an Italian word meaning one's optimum vocal range.

Let's say that a song has a range of ten notes, starting with middle C and extending to E, ten notes above middle C. Let's also assume that song is published in the key of C Major. What if the singer's best range lies in the area of the A flat below middle C to the C above middle C? It would be asinine for the singer to struggle with notes he or she does not sing easily. By transposing the song down three notes into the key of A flat major, the lower and upper notes of the song now coincide with the singer's optimum range. That is all there is to the art of transposing as far as the performer is concerned. The pianist will have to either transpose the song at sight, or change the chord symbols to facilitate the transposition. That's why it makes sense for the actor/singer to invest the money to have the song recopied in the new key. It is not frightfully expensive: It will cost you less than $10.00 a page to get a complete piano-vocal arrangement transposed and copied. Since the average copy of sheet music is three to four pages in length, the total cost should run about $35.00—not a luxury when you stop to realize that three or four good songs should serve your audition needs for years to come.

Usually the piano arrangements of great songs are terrible. The chords and harmonies are unsophisticated, to say the least, and do little to enhance your performance. However, a good accompanist can usually not only play what's written but can read from the chord symbols found on most published sheet music and add missing harmonies and fills.

If you have rotten luck with the accompanists provided for you at auditions, do not be afraid to bring in your cassette recorder with your accompaniments taped the way you are used to hearing them played. I will discuss this, and other tactics for survival at auditions, in Chapter 12.

To Rewrite or Not To Rewrite

At some point in your auditioning career you'll probably come up against the question of rewriting lyrics. There are many wonderful Cole Porter songs, for example, that can no longer be sung because Porter was in the habit of using topical references to people and events that sometimes date the material terribly. A clever rewrite of a lyric or two can change all that and make the lyric and song usable again. I am all for it, even though there are purists who would be violently opposed to the whole idea. Of course, the finished product has to be as good (or almost as good) as the original.

In a lovely George and Ira Gershwin song called "Isn't It a

Pity," the release to the chorus is cute but contains topical references that I feel are a bit precious today—rhyming "off in China" with "reading Heine," and "fishing for salmon" with "backgammon." They were fine fifty years ago. I changed the release to

> Imagine all the lonely years we wasted;
> Missing a fond rhyme with no Stephen Sondheim.
> What joys untasted;
> You reading Albee. I could not a pal be . . .

Before you cry heresy!, let me assure you that when students of mine sing this at an audition they are greeted with more attention than they received when they sang it as written. If Ira Gershwin had his options, and he were alive today, he would revise his lyrics and update them himself.

Another instance in which the actor may rewrite, if he possesses the skill, is when there is not enough lyric and the chorus is too short. A song that comes to mind is Rodgers and Hart's "Nobody's Heart," which is a very short, thirty-two bar ABAB song. The verse comes out of plotline so it is totally unusable. The interlude is all about Amazons riding (so was the show, more or less), so it is of no possible use to any actor in an audition situation. Yet the song is a gem whose one fatal flaw is that it is too short. To remedy this, so it could be used by one of my students, I imitated Larry Hart's style and wrote an additional release and final eight measures. Here is the result.

> Without a hand to hold;
> Nobody holds my hand,
> And yet it's grand, I'm told
> To wear a wedding band.
>
> Nobody's lips are pressing mine.
> No hand's caressing mine.

I admire a star
From afar—there you are.
Nobody's heart belongs to me today.

When my students sing the extra release and final eight
measures at an audition, even the most seasoned writers, directors, and lyricists swear that my students have discovered additional unpublished Lorenz Hart lyrics. Let them continue to
think that.

As long as the material is going to be used only in an audition
situation, I see nothing wrong in rewriting or writing additional
lyrics. If it means that a beautiful song, one that might have
never been used today because of certain limitations, can now
be sung again, I'm all for it.

A Change of Gender

A question I'm often asked is whether men can sing women's
songs and women sing men's songs. I think it is an excellent
idea as long as the number is not a love song that mentions the
name of the beloved. Obviously a man can't sing "Bill" from
Showboat, and a woman couldn't sing "Once in Love with Amy"
from *Where's Charlie*, but short of that, I see nothing wrong with
changing gender. It gives a tired song a whole new slant.
Hearing a man sing "The Trolley Song" from *Meet Me in St.
Louis,* or a woman sing "Tonight at Eight" from *She Loves Me!*
would be very refreshing, and I bet it would make auditors sit
up and take notice.

Sometimes changing the gender of a song can lead to fine
comedy. I remember rewriting the lyric of "I Guess I'll Have to
Change My Plan" by Howard Dietz and Arthur Schwartz from
The Bandwagon for one of my female students, who needed a
sophisticated comedy song to sing.

The song of course was written for a man who finds that the

female object of his planned seduction is already married. The original goes like this:

I Guess I'll Have To Change My Plan

(verse)
I beheld her, and was conquered at the start
And placed her on a pedestal apart.
I planned the little hide-away
That we would share some day.

When I met her I unfolded all my dreams
And told her how she'd fit into my schemes
Of what bliss is. Then the blow came
When she gave her name as Mrs.

(chorus)
I guess I'll have to change my plan,
I never realized there was another man.
I overlooked that point completely
Before the big affair began.
Before I knew where I was at
I found myself upon the shelf
And that was that.
I thought I'd reach the moon, but when I got
  there
All that I could get was the "air."
My feet are back upon the ground.
I lost the one girl I found.

With a slight change of a few lines, look how well it works for a woman. I should note that the verse basically stayed the same except for changing "her" to "him" in the first line, and in the last line where I exchanged "When she gave her name as Mrs."

---

for "What a situation this is!" in order to make it feminine. Here is the new lyric of the chorus.

> I guess I'll have to change my plan.
> I never guessed that he preferred another man.
> I overlooked that point completely
> Before the big affair began.
> I'm disillusioned, and perplexed.
> He's left me high and dry, now I am oversexed.
> Although I must confess this mixture was strong,
> He liked my features, yes, but the fixtures were
>   wrong.
> I'll have to change my plan today.
> I picked the wrong man . . . he's gay!

My student made quite a hit whenever she sang this number at my lecture-demonstration classes. Although some purists will grumble at my effrontery in rewriting a classic like this, the important point I wish to make is that the song has gained new life and is now usable by women. All is fair in love and war, and auditioning, after all.

Head or Chest—What Register Is Best?

The "belt" voice has long been an enigma to those who don't have one. As far as I know, the United States is the only country where it is used in the musical theatre.

In opera there are many different categories of voices such as coloratura, soprano, dramatic soprano, mezzo, and contralto for women and counter-tenor, lyric tenor, tenor, lyric baritone, bass baritone, bass, and basso profundo for men. In comparison, the musical theatre recognizes only four: soprano, chest or belt, tenor, and baritone. Occasionally basses are needed for character roles, such as Jud in *Oklahoma*. The voice that is most in demand for men is the baritone voice. The voice most commonly required for women is a good soprano. The terms *head voice* and *soprano* are used interchangeably, as are *chest voice* and *belt*. In many musical audition situations women are expected to use both their upper and lower registers. They are usually asked for a "belt" number and a "legit" number. I'll discuss how the belt voice came about in the first place a little later on in this chapter, but for now it is important to know that it is a forceful use of a woman's chest voice. It is produced in the larynx by powerful vibrations of the vocal cords which are resonated by bones and cartilage in the larynx only. Larynxes that have the right cartilage and bone formations to resonate the belt voice are a rarity, a sort of accident of nature. That is why Merman and other belters are such a rare phenomenon. Other cavities produce the resonances that create beautiful soprano tones and the overtones that give different singers their unique sound. The more resonation, the more soundwaves to hit the ear of the listener.

Many women who possess both strong sopranos and strong lower registers often ask me how to tell if a song should be belted, sung "in chest," or sung in the soprano register. There are a few guidelines one can follow.

1. If you are singing a blues number or a lament of an earthy nature use the chest voice (lower register).

2. If you are singing a fast up-number with lots of plosives in the lyric, like "The Trolley Song" or "Johnny One Note," use the lower register and belt it.

3. If you are singing a song that is ingenue in feeling, or one that shows vocal range better suited to using a higher vocal tessitura, then by all means use the "head" voice (soprano).

4. If the song is limited in range, that is, if it has a tessitura of an octave or less, keep it in the chest voice.

WHY THE BELT VOICE IS USED

Years ago, around the turn of the century, huge monster-sized theatres for musical productions were built on Forty-second Street in New York City. These theatres, such as The New Amsterdam (which still remains), could accommodate several thousand people in buildings the size of opera houses.

The musical productions of that time were no more than Viennese or English imports of light operetta fare. The small soprano voices of the typical casts of those days could not possibly fill the house, and it was impossible to hear the lyrics. Remember that there were no microphones and no electronic amplification in those days, so voices were needed that allowed for every syllable to be heard.

Since the belt voice is in the chest register, and the chest register is an extension of the speaking voice in its conversational tonal range, it was the ideal voice to fill these behemoths of theatres. It finally became a tradition that the Broadway musical should be synonymous with the belt voice coming from chorus girls and leading ladies who were lucky enough to have one. There is nothing as explosive and exciting as a good belt sound, under the right conditions and circumstances. It is like the excitement of hearing the brass in a Broadway overture.

VOCAL DICTION AND THE HEAD AND CHEST VOICES

It doesn't seem reasonable that language should be clearer in the lower register and obscured in the upper register of a woman's voice, yet it is. Remember that the chest, or lower register of a woman's voice, is the same register she has been using to speak in since she was a child. We are all taught to speak by rote. We first learned by listening to our parents and others. I doubt if any of us were formally taught how to pronounce vowels, dipthongs, tripthongs, plosives, liquids, and fricatives when we were learning how to talk. Therefore the chest voice already functions perfectly in the vocal extension of speech. The soprano voice is another story.

When we speak there is a definite ratio or relationship to two very different, distinct forms of energy that we employ. First, there is the automatic production of sound that comes from breath, the air vibrating the vocal cords as they resist it. Second, there is the energy that also produces sound that comes from using the tongue, the teeth, the lips, and the palate to produce consonants, plus the position of the throat used to shape the vowels. These two have to be kept in perfect relationship to one another if good, clean, discernable verbal sounds are going to result.

To prove my point, just think of the last time you heard someone try to speak who had drunk way too much alcohol. Wasn't the speech slurred and difficult to understand? What happened was that the alcohol had dulled and overly relaxed the muscles that control the tongue and lips, resulting in speech that was somewhat indistinguishable. In other words, that precious balance of the two distinct forms of vocal energy, which we have just discussed, has been changed.

When someone is singing in the soprano register something very similar happens: the balance between vibration of sound and the formation of consonants is also thrown out of sync. Why? Because the higher one sings, the more vocal energy to produce language has to be used. The higher one sings, the more support and breath control are needed to vibrate the vocal cords. To balance this vocal energy greater force and attention have to be given to activating the tongue, teeth, lips, throat, and palate to form lip consonants, plosives, liquids, and fricatives. Once the singer thoroughly increases this emphasis, to the point of exaggeration, the soprano voice will be as clear and as forceful as the chest voice. Part of the reason some singers are reluctant to do this is that they have been mistaught by their voice teachers to sing only on the vowel. This disregards the fact that the English language employs consonants far more often than just vowels.

In my classes I have continually had to do remedial work on vocal diction. It is a joy when, all of a sudden, students who once cracked on certain notes are producing beautifully clear and articulate sounds and words.

When the art of singing is properly understood, and properly taught, there is no discernable break in the registers of the voice to the ears of the listener.

4

Presentation

In performing a song in the context of a musical, an actor has the following things working for him:

1. His song is coming out of plot line and character development, so the audience already cares about him.

2. He is playing to an acting partner who is either onstage with him or is implied by the script. Sometimes the audience becomes a surrogate alter ego, and it may become the acting partner.

3. The actor is in costume and is made up as the character.

4. The actor has lights, scenery, and an orchestra to help make his performance more believable.

5. The actor has a curtain that can open and close to help define beginnings and endings of scenes.

It is quite apparent that the actor has *none* of these things going for him in an audition situation. He does, however, have his body which, if used properly, can take the place of what is lacking at a musical audition. In this chapter, we will take a close look at the physical elements of an audition performance, and see how you can put them all together and make them work for *you*.

The Eyes Have It

If I were to ask any actor or actress what was the most important thing they had going for them in an audition situation I would probably be told it was the voice, the material, the attire, the monologue, anything but the real truth. The most important thing an actor has working for him, and the one thing that is most misused, if it is used at all, is the *eyes*.

We have all heard the old bromide, "The eyes are the windows of the soul." Well, take my word for it. The eyes *are* the most expressive, hypnotic, compelling, and captivating part of the human anatomy. If they weren't, the US cosmetics industry wouldn't be taking in more than a billion dollars a year just for eye makeup alone. What woman today does not own false eyelashes, mascara, and eyeliner? What actor does not use theatrical makeup onstage?

The contact lens industry flourishes because millions of people realize the importance of making eye contact, especially where romance and sexual attraction are concerned. We know that people *hide* behind tinted lenses and sunglasses. Some find these concealing glasses sexy because there is a certain sexuality in being mysterious.

So why is it that actors do not know how to use their eyes at auditions? The answer is simple: they've never been taught. In commercial courses they are taught how and how not to play to the camera. In soap opera acting courses they are taught how to make the camera an acting partner, and in scene study they are taught how to play to an acting partner. But at musical auditions the actor is usually in a quandary. He does not know where or when to look, or who to look at.

If you could sit in on some musical auditions you would see some of the following things taking place:

1. *The actor is singing to no one in particular,* therefore his eyes are rolling around in his head. The result is that he is literally repelling the people he wishes to attract. They are turning away from him because he is like one of those disturbed people we see on the subway or sidewalk who are talking to themselves.

2. *The actor is playing and looking directly at one or more of the people he is auditioning for and making direct eye contact with them.* Here the result is the same. The people auditioning him will look away from him. Why? Imagine how you would feel if a stranger on the bus, subway, or street stared at you. You would either look away or haul off and belt him one. No one wants his privacy invaded by a stranger.

   We are a nation of voyeurs. Everyone sort of wants to look but not be looked back at in return. (Thus the popularity of mirrored sunglasses.) People who are casting a show are there to *look* at talent. They are buyers; they have a right to look. You gave them this right by showing up at the audition in the first place. You do not have the same right. Besides, the people auditioning you are not your acting partner or partners. If it is a love ballad you are singing, imagine how ludicrous it is singing it to an unappealing stranger of the same sex. Even if your auditioner is not of the same sex, if you play a song to them in a personal way, it could be interpreted as a seductive gesture that will cost you the audition before you have even half finished.

   The *only* time you can make eye contact with strangers in a musical performance is when you are singing in a nightclub. There at least the customers have paid for the privilege, and the booze and environment make it *safe* for you to do so. An audition situation will never provide you with that safety unless you know personally all the people you are auditioning for and they are close friends of yours. Even then you preclude their seeing you objectively. You might even be hindering yourself from getting a job you might have gotten otherwise.

3. *The actor is staring out in space at no one in particular.* You might as well be watching a zombie or mannequin with a built-in loudspeaker in its navel. After a few measures there is no reason in the world to continue watching this performance or performer. It's a mercifully quick "Thank you!"

What, then, should you do with your eyes? How do you use them? First let us define what is taking place at a musical audition. The actor sings a song, and (one hopes) acts it while he is singing it. To begin with, what is a song under these circumstances? *A song is a musical scene where we only hear one half of the dialogue occurring between two or more people.*

Now we see why there has to be an acting partner for you at the moment you are ready to sing your song. Obviously, you can't bring a real live person with you to an audition, but you can do the next best thing. You can bring an *invisible* acting partner that you will place at the back of the room or at the rear of the theatre. You do not have to play to the people auditioning you in order to have their attention. As I said, we are a nation of voyeurs; we are also a nation of people intrigued by other people looking at things. If one person is looking in a store window he'll soon attract a group of others milling around doing the same thing.

Once we know that an invisible acting partner (or *spot*, which is the technical term) is needed to make a song come to life, we can go through our mental files to pick the appropriate acting partner for the song we want to perform. If it is a love song, we are not going to put our dentist at the back of the room. The acting partner must be someone we are comfortable with. In this respect, the actor/singer has an advantage over the dramatic actor in audition situations, because he will not be stuck with an acting partner who is not of his own choosing.

SPOTTING

Put your acting partner on the back wall at your eye level, so that you are playing five or six inches over the heads of the people you are singing for. Pick the person in the *center* of the group and spot over his or her head. That way everyone will be able to see your face, and especially your eyes, and the feeling will be that you are playing *toward* them and not *to* them.

One other caution that I have to mention: under no circumstances should you close your eyes while you are singing. You may feel more protected if you do, but you will shut your audience out completely. They will not care one iota about you.

Turning a spot on the wall into a believable, live person takes practice and time. Here's an exercise that I require of my students in class and also in my private coaching. Find a picture, poster, or any physical object that is about eye level hanging on your wall. Practice visualizing someone you know and putting him or her where that spot is. Talk to that person. Argue with him or her. Put several different people there in turn. Start with your parents, then brothers and sisters, friends, lovers, enemies, and spouses in turn. *Don't forget to blink.* People always do when they first try this. The more believable you make your acting partner, the more believable you will be. Do all the things you would normally do in conversation or in a scene with an acting partner. Try this for five minutes a day for a week or so and you will be a pro.

Hands and Arms

After the eyes, the arms are the most important part of the body that the actor possesses. Unfortunately, they are also, again, one of the most misused. At any musical audition you will see one actor/singer after another just standing there with his arms at his sides. Nothing could be more boring, nothing could be more lifeless.

Hands are one of the most expressive tools an actor has to work with. You would never think of playing a scene or delivering a monologue with your arms at your sides, yet for some unfathomable reason you might think it seems perfectly all right to sing a song that way. Music can mask a multitude of sins, but arms at the sides is not one of them. Failing to use your arms and hands at a musical audition is more than foolish; it will cost you the job. You will appear lifeless and dull within four measures no matter how beautiful your voice might be.

How, then, to avoid this problem? Where should your arms and hands be while you are performing? When you are not using them to act or illustrate you should hold them lightly together in front of you below waist level. This should be considered *neutral*, very much like neutral in a car's gearshift. From neutral you can go to first, then second, even up to fourth or fifth. In acting a song this would correspond to raising your arms higher and higher. Reverse would be the equivalent of lowering your arms, until they are finally at your sides. This should only occur at the moment that the song is over. There is a certain limited area in which the arms and hands can be used safely when a *conversational* statement is being acted/sung. In order to find this area, stand up and touch your elbows to your side and keep them there. Now with the rest of each arm describe a circle. You can use your arms as freely as you want as long as you stay in this area. Of course, if the acting beat is strong enough, and you are no longer acting conversationally, you may use your arms in a much larger way without worrying about upstaging yourself. We will discuss the timing on all this a bit later in the chapter.

Hands produce a simple kind of body language when they are used unconsciously. Hands on the hips have a hostile connotation. You almost seem to be saying, "How long are you idiots going to keep me waiting here?" Arms folded at chest level are very defensive and seem to say, "Don't you dare get any closer!" Hands at the side when used as an acting beat mean "I have nothing to hide," or "I have nothing left to say, I am drained," and, finally, "It's all over."

The major reason that actors leave their arms at their sides is that they have never been taught to act with them. The problem also stems from the fact that they have learned their songs by rote and the lyric has never become a script to them. They stand with their arms down at their voice lessons, when they are vocalizing, so they stand the same way in performance at an audition. Mistake, mistake. They should reread this book and get themselves to a decent performance class *immediately*.

I hear many of my students say to me when confronted about this, "But I see actors in musicals standing there singing with their arms at their sides!" I then have to reply, "In a musical the actor is usually lit by a follow spot that lights him from waist level to above the head during a number. If it is a pinspot number, the actor is lit only from the shoulders up. The arms and hands are not visible under these circumstances."

I personally believe that many actors are not directed to use their arms and hands because directors who *stage* musicals today (that's all they really do) have a hard time getting a dramatic performance from most actors. The majority of directors who do musicals are choreographers turned directors, so if the number isn't a dance production number, you can expect this problem to show up.

The Performance, from Start to Finish

All art is a balance between tension and relaxation, says Ernest Toch, the composer and author. Art is also in part a study of the relationship of opposites. In music it is the relationship of melody to rhythm, of harmony to counterpoint, of consonance to dissonance, of loud to soft, and of sound to silence. In architecture, it is the relationship of vertical to horizontal and straight to curved. In modern dance, to quote Martha Graham, it is the contrast of contraction to release.

In the audition situation, it is the use of opposites and contrasts, the little physical and emotional adjustments, that will create the illusion that there is something there that isn't really there. Picasso says that art is lies that tell the truth. Nowhere is this more true than in stage design, wherein a designer, by use of foreshortening, the laws of perspective, and contrast of shading and color, can create the illusion of size and space where none exist.

MAKING YOUR ENTRANCE

The first thing that happens at a musical audition is that the performer must make an entrance either into the studio where the audition is taking place or onto the stage, if the audition is being held in a theatre. This entrance should be rehearsed and practiced to within an inch of your life.

Why? Very simple! While you are reading this you are in a relaxed state and probably saying, "This is ridiculous! Why should I rob myself of spontaneity by rehearsing the way I walk into a room?" The reason is simply that people are not spontaneous when they are filled with fear and facing a situation where they are being judged. Under these circumstances most people will not walk normally. Their faces will not be as relaxed as they normally are, and they will not be as free or as comfortable as they normally are under more relaxed circumstances. To create the illusion that he or she is relaxed, an actor literally has to act the part of someone who is. In my performance and audition classes I spend a good part of one class, at least, forcing people to practice making an entrance.

There are several exercises that I have devised for my students to give them the look of poise, relaxation, and self-acceptance when they make an entrance. The first is for those who compensate for their discomfort and fear of auditioning by walking in stiffly. Usually they come in looking as severe, cold, and rigid as a West Point cadet. They need to give themselves some mental adjustment that will defuse this stiffness.

Relaxation Exercise #1

Pretend that you are walking into a room of people who need your warmth and affection and who could not possibly threaten you in the least. Imagine that you are coming to meet and entertain crippled children, the disabled, or a group of senior citizens. Smile at them as you walk in. Project and radiate all the warmth you can muster.

Practice this exercise daily until you can turn this acting adjustment on and off whenever you want. Remember, a good audition is a rehearsed, top-notch performance that looks spontaneous, but can be summoned at will.

Relaxation Exercise #2

The second exercise was created for students who have such feelings of insignificance and inferiority at auditions that they walk in looking down at the floor, with never enough courage to even peek at the people who are auditioning them. They come in slumped over with the air of defeat written all over them. They need an adjustment that puts them in control of the situation, that gives them exactly the opposite look.

Before you make your entrance, take a moment and imagine yourself as owning the building and studio that the rehearsals are being held in. If your audition is taking place onstage, pretend that you are the landlord of the theatre. Take this even one step further: Imagine how you would feel if the people holding these auditions were delinquent and owed you three months' back rent. How would you walk in then? Would you still be threatened by them and their crummy auditions? Practice this exercise till you can turn on a sense of authority and power at will.

WHILE YOU'RE GETTING THEIR ATTENTION

After you have made your entrance, you may have to stall for time until you have the attention of the people auditioning you. It is foolish to nod to the pianist to start playing, and even more foolish for you to rush into a performance before you have your listeners' attention merely because you feel uncomfortable standing there.

The probable reason for your discomfort is that nothing is going on. By that I mean that if you are standing there like a department store dummy, of course you are going to look and feel odd. If you were standing at a bus stop or on a street corner waiting for a friend, you wouldn't be standing like a statue, would you? Of course not! You would be looking around at store windows, casually noticing other people or street signs, visually taking in anything that could possibly capture your momentary attention.

You would probably not be standing bolt upright, but would be "sitting" on one hip with one leg slightly bent and extended. Your hands would most likely be involved in some casual unconscious activity such as straightening your hair or your tie and jacket. Perhaps your fingers might be "playing" with a ring or a locket, or adjusting a sleeve or collar.

There are undoubtedly other adjustments that you can make while standing there waiting for someone's attention. Find those that feel and look natural on you. As long as these adjustments do not make you look like you are uncomfortable or nervous, by all means make them.

How will you know when you have the attention of those people you are auditioning for? You can see them out of the corner of your eyes. If they are looking forward at you, you know that it is now time to proceed to the next step, which is to nod to the pianist so that he can start playing the musical introduction to your song. Be sure you tell him in advance *not* to dare play a note until you give him the signal. If he starts to play before your nod it will throw your entire performance off.

In case that does happen, stop! Tell him again to wait for your nod and start again.

Why is this nod so desperately important? Because at some time during the playing of your introduction you are going to make a physical and emotional transition and transformation, from the person who just walked in to audition to the person who is now the leading character of the song you are singing. You can't do this if the pianist starts the introduction, or vamp as it sometimes is called, before you are ready.

THE PHYSICAL TRANSITION— HOW IT IS ACCOMPLISHED

Songs can start in one of two ways:

- The song may start *ad lib*, in which case the actor doesn't start singing, or acting, until after the pianist has played the introduction. This introduction usually ends on a held chord, the slang musical term used for which is "sting."

- The song starts *in tempo* (has a definite rhythmical beat), in which case the actor would let half the musical introduction go by before he starts to make his physical transition and begins acting the song. In a song that is in tempo you can always ask the pianist to double the introduction if it isn't long enough to allow you to make the physical transition that the opening line requires.

Remember where we spoke in detail about the use of "contrasts" of opposites in creating the illusion of a definite performance? Here is where the first illusion takes place—in making the transition from *you* waiting there to sing to *you* going into character and performance. We accomplish this by means of a change in what the eyes are doing and in the way we are standing.

Until now, the eyes have not been focused on anything in particular. After the pianist has played the introduction, and it is time to go into character and start our performance, our eyes must find our imaginary acting partner. Since we must make this entity seem real not only to ourselves but to the people we are performing for, we must place our imaginary acting partner at a spot at about eye level to us and extending directly in front of us to the rear wall (as I have already described).

The effect of our eyes finding and zeroing in on our acting partner is the equivalent of the curtain going up. After this, the next adjustment we must make is in changing the way we are standing, going from that relaxed, casual, one-knee-bent, broken-hip stance to a "pulled up," at-attention position. These two adjustments follow each other very closely and very smoothly. They should not take place simultaneously. They are then followed by one last adjustment before the actor can finally start to sing—playing the "acting beat."

The acting beat is a physical and emotional adjustment involving the hands, arms, face, and rest of the body. Physicalizing the acting beat creates a climate that justifies, and is conducive to, the singing of the first line of the lyric. If a picture is worth a thousand words, so is an acting beat. It always tells the truth about how you really feel toward your acting partner, or about what you are saying.

The reason for these adjustments—eyes, stance, and acting beat—is that these three things (always in the order given) *always* happen in a real-life situation. Suppose you were walking down the street, saw your best friend looking into the display window of a department store, and called his name? Because your friend heard his name called he would turn his head to see the person who just addressed him. Only because he recognizes you will his eyes be focused on you. Some sort of relationship exists between you (after all, you are not strangers). Because of this relationship your friend's stance will change. If he was in a pulled-down position, he will now pull up. In other words, the fact that he is pleased to see you will have to be reflected in the way he is standing. Next, he will smile, extend his hand, or physically show how he feels about you. This reaction to seeing you is his acting beat.

Let's illustrate the techniques we have learned so far by analyzing what could happen if we applied it to a few songs:

Ten Cents a Dance

(Gladys, waiting to audition, is standing in a pulled-up position. Her eyes are casually taking in the room. Her hands have been casually straightening her hair, tucking in her blouse, and straightening her skirt. Noticing that she now has the attention of the people she is performing for, she nods to the accompanist, who gives her a very free, ad lib introduction that ends in a sustained chord (sting). While he is sustaining this chord, Gladys's eyes focus front on her imaginary acting partner, in this case a friend. As soon as she has focused on her friend, Gladys pulls downward into a more relaxed, laid-back way of standing. She sighs as her body goes into a limp, tired stance. Her arms go slightly out to convey the bitterness and frustration of what she is feeling as she sings:)

I work at the palace ballroom.
And gee that palace is cheap.

The reason that Gladys started in a pulled-up position before making her transition is that the song demands the performer to be pulled down to reflect the exhaustion of the character, who has just been on a seven-to-midnight stint of being a dance-hall hostess.

It's a Nice Face

(Bob is waiting to audition and standing in a pulled-down position, one hip broken with his weight on one foot, the other leg slightly bent and slightly extended in

*front of him. He has been stalling for time, waiting for
the attention of the people he is auditioning for. To give
himself a relaxed look he has been straightening his tie
and adjusting his jacket. When he notices that he has the
attention of his audience he nods to the accompanist. He
is given a four-bar, ad lib intro that ends in a sting.
While the sting is being sustained by the pianist Bob
plays forward, focusing his eyes on a spot on the back
wall. He then pulls up into an upright stance. Now he
strokes his chin quizzically, takes a moment to evaluate
what he has just seen, and sings:)*

It's a nice face
*(After a beat, in which he shrugs his shoulders slightly
he continues:)*
As faces go, it's a very nice face.

If the change in the eyes was the equivalent of "Curtain
going up!" then the equivalent for change of stance would be
"Lights!" and that of the acting beat, "Action!"

Where and When To Move in a Song

We are now into the body of the song. If the number had a
verse there will always be a move downstage from the verse to
the chorus. When we discussed the "in-one number" in Chapter
3, we learned how the practice of cheating downstage from the
verse into the chorus evolved. The move downstage is the first
and the only time this can occur in a song. If the song you are
singing does not have a verse you will have to move downstage
after the first eight-measure section, or A section, of the song.

There are two more places where you should move in a song:
to the side, either left or right of center, and from there back to
center again. Since you have already moved downstage from
the verse to the chorus it would be silly to move downstage

again. If you did you would be smack on top of your audience. The only sensible solution is a move to the side.

The place to do this is, first, between the second eight and the release, and second, between the end of the release and the final eight. These are usually places where you are holding a sustained note and they most often occur at the end of a section. Since the text has stopped momentarily, you are in danger of losing the attention of your audience. The empty space is too long to fill with just an acting beat, so be sure to move.

Why fill them at all? Because your audience at an audition is much different from your audience at a nightclub or theatre. The people auditioning you don't really want to be there at all. They are there only because they are casting a show and have to sit through hearing and watching over a hundred people a day. They are much like hostile witnesses in a courtroom; they have to be handled in a special way. In this instance, the special way consists of never letting them take their attention from you for a moment. You do this by *moving* and creating some sort of physical life in those empty spaces between complete sections of your song.

When I was going through adolescence in the early 1950s, we had had our first television set for only a few years. WNET, also known as Channel 13 in New York, started broadcasting. Since it was an educational TV network it did not have much money and could afford only one TV camera to start with. I had to practically force myself to watch the live dramas that they broadcast even though they starred famous actors and actresses. Why? Because I had a short attention span, and it was monotonous to see only one angle shot repeated over and over again. This I find akin to an actor standing in only one place during a song at an audition. He might be able to get away with it onstage in a performance because he has lighting effects and other visual interest going for him, but I'm willing to bet even there that unless he *and* the song are spectacular he will hear coughing and programs rattling in the empty spaces between sections of the song.

In moving to the side, you have to be very careful that while you're walking you don't turn your body in such a way that you lose the commitment and attention of your imaginary acting partner. If this happens you will lose the attention of your audience as well.

To avoid this, move sideways while facing front. This can easily be accomplished by shifting your weight onto the foot that is in the direction you want to go. If you want to move to the right then shift your weight onto your right foot. Once your weight is on that foot, move the other foot in front of it. This means that if you are moving to the right, the right foot will be behind and the left foot will be in front, and both feet will keep that relationship to one another until the move is completed. This requires practice to be executed smoothly. When done properly, the attention of the audience will never go down to your feet and the walk will be more felt than noticed.

Let's briefly review where the moves occur in an AABA song that has a verse. The first move is a walk downstage that lasts from the end of the verse to the beginning of the first word or two of the first eight of the chorus. The second move, which is from downstage center to either side, occurs at the end of the second eight. It starts on the last few words of the second eight and lasts until the first word or so of the release. The third, and usually the last, move occurs on the last word or two of the release and continues through the first word or so of the final eight.

Although these moves are mechanical, you should find organic reasons, coming out of the script (lyric) or subtext, that would justify them or at least make them dramatically believable.

There remains one more physical, or I should say mechanical, adjustment that you must execute before you can successfully complete the song, and that is the "ride out." *Ride out* is a musical term that describes the particular music that the orchestra or pianist is playing while you are singing and holding the last note of the song. When used to describe what you are doing during this time, ride out means what you elect to do physically to sustain visual interest in yourself while the last note of the song is being sung and sustained. It must last until the final note of the piano accompaniment has died away. Here's how to execute it.

First, define what you would want the director to tell the lighting man to do while you are singing the end of the song. Would there be a blackout? A slow fade? Your body can take the place of any of these effects if used correctly. The secret lies in the use of the hands and arms. Since we want the arms to be at the sides at the end of the song, we purposely get them up, just a little before the end of the song, so they can come down slowly while we are sustaining the final note and word. If the song were a ballad, the hands and arms would start coming down at a point no higher than chest height. If the song were an up-number, dynamically big and bright, then the arms would come down from a much higher starting position. Use the last line before the final note and word to get your arms up. Again, although the ride out is mechanical, do try to find a dramatic or subtextual reason for getting the arms up so you can time them down to the music.

The time has come to put all of this together and diagram and analyze a song from beginning to end. I have chosen "I Love My Wife," by that masterful composer Cy Coleman, with lyrics by Michael Stewart, for this example.

I Love My Wife

(Richard is standing in a large rehearsal hall about fifteen feet in front of the people he is auditioning for. He is standing in a pulled-down position. Since some of the people are still talking among themselves, and since the others are looking at pictures and resumés, it is quite clear to Richard that he isn't yet ready to nod to the pianist to begin playing his introduction. Richard fills

*the time by straightening his tie, tucking his shirt waist
into his slacks, and adjusting his jacket. He notices that
his audience is now silent and waiting for him to begin.
He nods to the accompanist who plays the written two-
measure introduction, which is in waltz time, twice.
Richard has told the pianist in advance to play it twice
because he needs that amount of time to make the transition and get into character.*

*Richard's eyes play center and see Elise, his imaginary
acting partner, on the back wall. This spot is at Richard's
eye level, and about a foot above the heads of the people
he is auditioning for. Seeing Elise, whom he loves
very much, he pulls up, reaches his arms to her and
sings:)*

My thoughts may stray,
(Shaking his head as if he is at a loss for words)
My eyes may roam,
(Somewhat apologetically)
**The neighbor's grass may seem much greener
Than the grass right here at home.**
(Looking toward her for some reassurance)
If pretty girls excite me, well, that's life.
(Interrupting her before she has a chance to protest)
**But just in case you didn't know,
I love my wife.**
*(On the last word of this first section, "wife," Richard
walks slowly downstage toward Elise, not stopping until
the first few words of the next section, "My mind at
times," are out of his lips. He holds out empty hands
toward her, as if he were slightly ashamed at what he is
about to say.)*
My mind at times
(Smiling sheepishly)

May dwell on sex.
(Almost hating to confess this)
If someone's rating dreams then most of mine
I guess are double X.
(Quite on the defensive)
So dimpled knees delight me,
Well, that's life.
(Richard looks away for a moment, refocuses his spot on Elise, rubs his hands in a slightly nervous manner as if what he's about to say is difficult for him.)
But just in case you hadn't heard,
I love my wife.
(On the words "My wife," Richard, never taking his eyes off Elise, moves to stage right, continuing the move through the words of the next section, "like bait," which are coming up. At the same time he chooses to play an acting beat that involves shrugging and moving his hands out to the side as he sings:)
Like bait that wriggles makes catfish bite,
(His eyes light up as he gets caught up in his fantasy.)
A lady jiggles
(Reaching out toward his fantasy)
And my eyes gotta light
Upon so sweet a sight.
(On the words "sweet a sight," Richard moves back to center, continuing the walk until the words, "and if I" have been sung by him. His new acting beat involves a change to an attitude of strength, happiness, and elation in the knowledge that she possibly understands and will accept his foibles.)
And if I shake, break out in spots,
(Almost laughing at the pun he is about to make)
Don't fret, it's not swine fever, dear,
Your swine has merely got the hots.
(Richard shrugs with a "what can you do" attitude.)
If rosy lips invite me, well, that's life.

(Richard brings his hands together, almost in the attitude of reverent prayer.)
But just in case you couldn't guess
(He starts to slowly raise his arms.)
Or hadn't heard or didn't know
(He extends his arms, reaching out for her.)
I love my wife.
(He extends his arms fully toward her, as far as they can go.)
I love my wife.
(On the third repeat of the words "I love my wife," starting on the word "wife," Richard's hands slowly come down, timing with the music until they are at his sides. This coincides with the last note of the accompaniment.)

EXITING FROM AN AUDITION PERFORMANCE

After the arms have come down, during the ride out, the performance is over. The next several moments are crucial. *Do not exit, walk away, or leave the spot you are standing in.*

What is happening at this time is that the people who have just auditioned you are deciding whether they are sufficiently interested in you either to hear you read, call you back, or ask you to sing a second song. If you move *before* they have made this decision you have preempted them, and they have no course but to let you depart or run after you. You would have to be little less than the Second Coming for that to happen.

Embarrassing as it might feel to you, stand there the way you did in the beginning of the song (when you were stalling for time) while you are waiting for their response. I know that no one wants to prolong a possible rejection, but rejecting a possible acceptance is a thousand times more self-defeating.

How To Handle a Callback

If your audition results in a callback, you should consider the following suggestions:

1. Sing exactly the same song or songs at the callback that you sang at the audition. They worked for you already. They will work for you again.

2. Wear exactly the same outfit that you had on initially. Do not change your hair style, or anything about the way you look, until *after* the callback.

3. If by chance they do request you sing something different at the callback, *remind* them of what you originally sang before proceeding. Sometimes in the confusion of seeing hundreds of people, you will be remembered only as the person in the red dress who sang that particular number. If you return not wearing the red dress, but wearing a blue one instead, and you are no longer singing that particular song, you've now become an unknown quantity as opposed to someone they've looked forward to seeing again.

4. Keep a diary, or else jot down in your appointment book, exactly what you sang, what you wore, and *whom* you sang it for. It is important to know the name of everyone who was there and who was interested in you. Those who like you may be in a position to give you a job in some future show at some future time. Many people are working on more than one project at a time. You could possibly luck into a job you weren't even auditioning for to begin with. Also, it doesn't hurt to keep a mailing list which will enable you to let these people know you're still alive and available.

How To Handle Yourself While Being Typed

In today's crowded audition situations, where there are more people waiting to be seen and heard than can possibly be accommodated, one must become accustomed to either being "typed in" or "typed out." This consists of standing in a line of from three to as many as sixteen competitors while the auditors decide who will sing, dance, and remain, and who will not. Usually during this process the would-be auditioners, praying for special dispensation from heaven, stand like statues, scared stiff and unsmiling. I recommend that you do what you usually do during your preparation to sing. Instead of standing there stiffly, smile, adjust your hair or clothing, and look around at your surroundings. You will be the only nonmannequin there. Remember we tend to hire and audition people, not mannequins. You will be way ahead of the game.

CHAPTER
5

How To Play a Comedy Song

Sooner or later every actor and actress worth his salt gets the bug and wants to play comedy. This is a wonderful desire, but most actors labor under the delusion that singing a funny song will automatically make them funny. Nothing could be further from the truth. Playing a comedy song requires that the performer know the basis for the comedy in the song. It *does not* require that the performer be funny.

There are many people around us who are naturally funny. Every word they utter seems to make us laugh or smile, and yet these same people die when they try to make comic material work. Why? Mainly because comedy is a craft. It has definite rules and techniques that can be deduced, learned, and taught. The natural sense of humor of these funny people has never been taken quite seriously by them. They have never analyzed it, therefore they don't know how to make it happen when they have to.

Being funny is not essential to making comedy work well. Nancy Walker, one of the greatest comediennes I have ever known, is also one of the most serious people I have ever met. And the legendary Fanny Brice was certainly one of the unhappiest performers. Some of our greatest comics and comediennes have been tragic figures. I remember the story of a middle-aged man who went to see a physician because he was suffering from such intense depression and crying jags that he was on the brink of ending it all. "You take life far too seriously," the physician told him. "You should go to the circus tonight and see the great Bertolini. He'll make you laugh and forget your depression." "But I *am* the great Bertolini!" exclaimed his patient sadly.

Part of the reason that some of our most successful comedy performers are tragic figures is that comedy and tragedy have the same common root, the reality of the human condition. You have to experience all conditions of life, or at least have an understanding of them, before you can play comedy or tragedy well. Exactly what are these conditions? Any and all aspects of living, including sex, love, death, naivete, distrust, taxes, religion, God, ethnicity, illegitimacy, incest, parents, children, political beliefs, business, competition, war, violence, rape, education, nature, sickness, blindness, deafness, birthdays, anniversaries, pets, success, failure, fame, obscurity—the list is endless.

Here is a master of comic songwriting, Murray Grand, using death, accidents, drugs, emphsyma, aging, anger, promiscuity, and alcoholism as the basis for a great comedy number. This song works best for someone just a little bit past the prime of life. The music is a sensual, torrid beguine.

Too Old To Die Young

Let me run in front of trucks,
Smash the mirror on my wall;
Let me puff away and choke,
Sniff a little coke
And have myself a ball.
After all I'm too old to die young.

Let me walk against the lights,
Let me drive when I am drunk;
Let me be a little hip,
Take a little trip
And try a little junk.
After all I'm too old to die young.

Let me pick up strangers in the street,
Sleep with everyone I meet;
Drink in dives along the docks,
Get the pox.

Let me stay a trifle stoned,
Who's to know and who's to care;
Let me find another thrill,
Pop another pill
And breathe polluted air.
Do I care if I'm minus a lung;
After all I'm too old to die young.

Let me wear my ankle strap shoes,
Fall in potholes if I choose;
If someone says that I'm a fright,
They may be right.

Let my face begin to fall,
Let it wrinkle like a prune;
Will I know my liver's gone
While I'm lying on
The floor of a saloon.

Give me speed, give me hash,
Let me fly, let me crash.
Let me sail, let me sink.
Lock me up in the clink.
Drop the bomb on my head,

> Not a tear will I shed,
> Not a moan, not a sigh,
> As I kiss my assets good-bye.
> What the hell! I'm too old
> To die young.

"Too Old To Die Young" epitomizes the clever humor that is the stock-in-trade of writers like Lorenz Hart, Cole Porter, Noel Coward, and Stephen Sondheim. Much of their humor is based upon plays on words as well as on double entendre. In "Too Old To Die Young" the basis for comedy is the exaggeration of a problem, namely aging. Stretching the truth, especially in the area of problems, is a perfect base for comedy writing. Brilliant examples of this technique can be found in well-known numbers from musicals such as "I Can't Say No" from *Oklahoma!* (Rodgers and Hammerstein), "Adelaide's Lament" from *Guys and Dolls* (Frank Loesser), "Shy" from *Once Upon a Mattress* (Mary Rodgers and Marshall Barrer), and "Why Can't a Woman Be More Like a Man?" from *My Fair Lady* (Lerner and Loewe).

In "I Can't Say No," Ado Annie has a problem that almost every woman and man in the audience can identify with: there have been times when they either didn't want to say no or they didn't want their partner to say no. What makes the number work in the context of the show is that Ado Annie is simultaneously bemoaning her problem and relishing it with extraordinary glee.

In "Shy," Winnefred laments the fact that she has always been shy while belting out that information to us in the most extroverted manner possible. In this example, of course, the song is a lie but it *must* be played for real. If there is no problem then there is no basis for this type of a comedy song, at least not a comedy song that will work.

In "Adelaide's Lament," Adelaide reads aloud from a book that describes how emotional stress and rejection can bring on all the psychosomatic symptoms of flu or, at the very least, a bad cold. As she is reading this aloud, and commenting on her own unhappy, frustrated emotional state, she starts exhibiting all of the symptoms she has been reading about.

In "Why Can't a Woman Be More Like a Man?" Alan Jay Lerner has taken Henry Higgins's problem (Eliza Doolittle bolting and his not comprehending her emotional turmoil or her feelings of rejection at being unappreciated) and turned it around into one of the greatest pieces found in musical theatre literature. Higgins, instead of trying to fathom Eliza's motives, launches into a tirade maximizing the virtues of men to the emotional faults he perceives in women. He uses the technique of presenting one-sided facts in a logical manner to prove an illogical point, namely that, overall, men are a marvelous sex.

Sometimes the basis of humor in a comedy song is not merely the exaggeration of a problem. Sometimes it lies in the heightened ridiculousness of a situation. This was the secret of W. S. Gilbert's successful comedy in all the Gilbert and Sullivan operettas. A perfect example of this can be found in the biographical narrative "When I Was a Lad," from *H.M.S. Pinafore*.

> **When I was a lad I served a term**
> **As office boy to an attorney's firm.**
> **I cleaned the windows and I swept the floor**
> **And polished up the handles of the big front**
> **   door.**
> **I polished up that handle so carefully**
> **That now I am the ruler of the Queen's navy!**

So far it seems impossible for an office boy in an attorney's firm to ever become an admiral. The humor of the song's premise is how this pompous windbag is about to fill in the missing steps.

"When I Was a Lad," from *H.M.S. Pinafore*. Lyrics by W. S. Gilbert, music by Sir Arthur Sullivan. Public Domain.

> As office boy I made such a mark
> That they gave me the post of a junior clerk.
> I served the writs with a smile so bland,
> And I copied all the letters in a big round hand.
> I copied all the letters in a hand so free
> That now I am the ruler of the Queen's navy.

He's gotten a step closer to his goal, but it still seems ludicrous. Note the satirical commentary on junior clerks.

> In serving writs I made such a name
> That an articled clerk I soon became;
> I wore clean collars and a brand new suit
> For the pass examination at the institute.
> That pass examination did so well for me
> That now I am the ruler of the Queen's navy.

He's getting up in the world of clerks but as yet is no closer to admiralcy. Notice the humorous importance placed upon a brand-new suit and a clean collar as the major reason for passing his examination.

> Of legal knowledge I acquired such a grip
> That they took me into partnership.
> And that junior partnership, I ween,
> Was the only ship that I have ever seen.
> But that kind of ship so suited me
> That now I am the ruler of the Queen's navy.

Here we have a play on the "ship" in partnership that sets up a marvelous put down of the bureaucratic system that promotes and appoints men to high office who are totally unfit.

> I grew so rich that I was sent
> By a pocket borough into Parliament.
> I always voted my party's call,

> And I never thought of thinking for myself at all.
> I thought so little, they rewarded me
> By making me the ruler of the Queen's navy.

This is the most scathing and politically satiric part of the song and contains the crux of his secret of success. This criticism of the system would have been considered sarcastic and inflammatory had it appeared in an essay written by Gilbert. In an operetta it becomes joyful political satire.

> Now landsmen all, whoever you may be,
> If you want to rise to the top of the tree,
> If your soul isn't fettered to an office stool,
> Be careful to be guided by this golden rule.
> Stick close to your desks and never go to sea,
> And you all may be the rulers of the Queen's
>   navy.

The simple secret of playing comedy songs effectively is to really give yourself over to the character you have elected to play. Since exaggeration is the basis for 90 percent of all comedy material, it does no good to hold back.

Even in clever numbers, where the lyric is really what makes us laugh, the performer *has* to overplay the character and the emotion the character is feeling. Some years ago I wrote the following song for Carol Burnett, which she performed on her Christmas shows for several years and which has become a comedy standard.

The Twelve Days After Christmas

> The first day after Christmas
> My true love and I had a fight,
> And so I chopped the pear tree down

"The Twelve Days After Christmas," lyrics and music by Fred Silver. © 1968 McAfee Music, a division of Belwin Music Publishing Corp. Used by permission.

And burned it, just for spite.
Then with a single cartridge
I shot that blasted partridge
My true love, my true love,
My true love gave to me.

The second day after Christmas
I put on some old rubber gloves
And very gently wrung the necks
Of both the turtle doves
My true love, my true love
My true love gave to me.

The third day after Christmas
My mother caught the croup,
And so I killed the three French hens
To make some chicken soup.

The four calling birds were a big mistake,
For their language was obscene.
And the five golden rings were completely fake
'Cause they turned my fingers green.

The sixth day after Christmas
The six laying geese wouldn't lay.
I gave the whole damn gaggle to
The ASPCA.

On the seventh day what a mess I found.
The seven swans a-swimming all had drowned
That my true love, my true love,
That my true love gave to me.

The eight day after Christmas
Before they could suspect
I bundled up the eight maids a-milking,
Nine pipers piping, ten ladies dancing,
Eleven lords a-leaping, twelve drummers drum-
    ming,

(spoken as an aside)
"Well actually, I kept one of the drummers."
And sent them back collect.

I wrote my true love, "We are through, love,"
And I said in so many words,
"Furthermore your Christmas gifts were for
The birds,
Four calling birds, three French hens,
Two turtle doves,
And a partridge up your pear tree!"

Obviously, the cleverness of the number doesn't lie solely in the fact that it is a parody of a well-known Christmas carol, but in the fact that the song tells us what she did with the gifts. The humor really comes from her hating her lover so much for having jilted her, supposedly after the fight, that she maliciously destroys all the gifts he gave her. The way she destroys them may or may not strike us as being funny, but her overblown and exaggerated anger should.

Sometimes comedy can be found in a situation where one is totally unaffected by an immoral act. The first example that immediately comes to my mind is Lorenz Hart's "To Keep My Love Alive" from *Connecticut Yankee*, where the singer calmly and gleefully tells us of the hordes of husbands she has murdered simply because she doesn't believe in divorce. The clever rhymes and images make this a well-written comedy number. But the song will work only if the performer thoroughly *enjoys* having dispatched all her husbands and *relishes* telling us graphically how each one died.

Stephen Sondheim tried to pull off the same sort of thing in "I Never Do Anything Twice," but only partially succeeded. His rhymes and images were predictable. For this reason the song remains a "personality number," one in which only the personality of a well-known, gifted performer can make the song work. The only performer who ever made it work for me was Hermione Gingold in the New York production of *Side by Side by Sondheim*.

The last type of comedy song I would like to present is the number that owes its humor to the embarrassment or humiliation felt by the acting partner who is the recipient of some abuse. We find it funny because we are identifying with the acting partner in much the same way that we laugh at the victim of one of Don Rickles's put downs, and then breathe a sigh of relief that it was not directed at us.

True Confession

(verse)
We've been friends for years and years,
First through pubescence,
Then adolescence, right up to now.
And I've never ever pried into your past, John,
But now at last, John,
I ask you how?
How could our friendship grow so close and so
   intense
When I've never really known you, at least
In the Biblical sense.

(chorus)
You've been intimate with all my friends and
   lovers.
At least they've intimated quite untactfully
That I'm the only one
Who hasn't joined the fun.
Yes, everybody's had you but me.

Last Christmas I was told by my dear mother
That on some drunken, wild weekend spree
You proceeded to seduce
My younger brother, Bruce.
Everybody's had you but me.

"True Confession" from *In Gay Company*, lyrics and music by Fred Silver. Copyright 1980 by Genesis III Music Corp., publisher. Used by permission.

Remember when we went to Mass and took our
     first Communion
You were in that damn confessional for hours.
And at least I found it odd
That that priest, a man of God,
Should send you that divine bouquet of flowers.

Your list of conquests makes "Who's Who" a
     memorandum.
No one else could manage a ménage à cinq
With my cousin Sam, the actor,
And our family chiropractor,
And two tellers that you picked up in the bank.

I've heard it rumored that you were bisexual
But tossed it off as just a lot of noise.
Now, though you haw and hem
I know you're one of them,
And bisexual means to you both men and boys.

I've felt slighted, and ignored, and quite rejected.
I would have told you sooner but was much too
     shy.
If my friends are good enough
For your romantic fluff
I ask you, John, why aren't I?

(She looks away coyly.)
Since I've admitted I adore you
I beseech you and implore you
To dispell this hell and tell me honestly
Why everybody's had you . . .
*(She turns around to look for him but he has slipped
away.)*
But me.

     To sum it all up, acting a comedy song requires exaggeration
of almost every acting technique we discussed in Chapter 2.

The physical gestures have to be larger in size than you would use in playing a noncomedy song, the emotions would have to be heightened, the diction would have to be articulated and emphasized more. Everything would have to be played in the most overt manner possible, as subtlety is often lost in comedy.

It is the obligation of the performer to reconstruct in his or her mind what is the basis for the song's humor, why the character is making that particular statement in the first place, and what dramatic devices and techniques will make the character come to life, larger than life itself.

An important consideration is that the true basis for comedy lies always in the character's needs, wants, fears, frustrations, and approach to life. When the lyricist's approach to life takes over and the performer is merely mouthing the lyricist's clever thoughts, we have a clever number that does little for the character or the actor playing that character. In writing the lyrics for "You've Gotta Have a Gimmick" in *Gypsy,* Stephen Sondheim created a brilliant comedy number, giving three tired, worn-out strippers their raison d'être for what they did and at the same time giving Gypsy Rose Lee her insight into what her gimmick was to be. When the character's reality is thrown out the window, however, it injures the musical and doesn't do a whole lot for the actor who is singing that particular song.

For audition purposes, I always admonish my students to beware of numbers with lyrics that are more clever than they are. No one ever became a star singing a Sondheim song. However, Carol Burnett's career certainly did take off when she sang "Shy" in *Once Upon a Mattress,* Vivian Blaine became a star after stopping *Guys and Dolls* cold with "Adelaide's Lament," and Barbra Streisand tore up the house in *I Can Get It for You Wholesale* with a simple comedy number, "Miss Marmelstein," lamenting the almost insignificant fact that no one could pronounce her name.

The first rule of comedy is, especially for audition purposes, always be better, or at least as good, as your material.

CHAPTER
6

Stage Fright!

If Sören Kierkegaard hadn't gotten there first, I would have loved to title this chapter "Fear and Trembling," "The Sickness Unto Death," and/or "The Concept of Dread." What better way to sum up the horrible problem that most actors have experienced at one time or another—stage fright.

Many of us are familiar with the symptoms of stage fright, although they can differ from person to person as to type and intensity. Some may experience nausea, stomach cramps, shortness of breath, dizziness, a throbbing in the temples, dry throat, dry mouth, excessive sweating, tremors, or shaking of the arms or legs, while others may experience a temporary memory loss or a strong sense of impending doom and disaster. I know many people who can't stop running to the bathroom, and I know others who have become so hysterical that I have had to shake them just to calm them down.

I have only experienced actual fullblown stage fright once in my life, just before I was about to perform at a concert at Lincoln Center. I was part of the duo-piano team of DeMaio and Silver. We had just finished a year's run at the Rainbow Room. Our speciality was playing show music and pop music the way Bach, Beethoven, Brahms, Chopin, Rachmanninoff, and all the other great composers might have written it. Every month, while we were at the Rainbow Room, we would do a salute to the music of some great living theatre composer. We did a Cy Coleman night, a Richard Rodgers night, a Stephen Sondheim night, a Lerner and Loewe night, plus many more too numerous to mention. When we would do a musical salute to these people, they would be there as guests of the Rainbow Room and the press would cover it.

The point is that most of these very same people were at our Lincoln Center concert, which was very well attended. When I began to feel the unfamiliar symptoms of stage fright taking hold of me I turned to my partner and told him I didn't think I could possibly go on. I will never forget what he said to me that stopped my panic cold. He said: "Idiot! . . . How can you be nervous when all those people out there paid good money to see us do what they *can't* do." He was absolutely right, and I was never frightened again in any performance situation.

The feeling that had overtaken me was a fear of being judged and found wanting. My partner was able to neturalize that fear, alleviating the stage fright as quickly as it had begun. Since there are many different fears and other subtle causes of stage fright, let's see if we can't examine them and figure out a way to neutralize them, rob them of their power, and prevent them from happening again.

The Fear of Being Judged and Being Found Wanting

This fear is neutralized by *not giving your would-be judge or judges that power in the first place.* True, they may be in a position to give you a job, but that will happen *only* if they can use you. They may judge you to be a marvelous talent, but if you are not right for a role there is no earthly way you are going to get hired. The truth is that we are really never being judged in any situation outside of a court of law. All the judging is being done by ourselves. There is so much truth in the Biblical admonition "Judge not lest ye be judged." People who are self-judgmental are usually people who are highly critical of others. They don't accept themselves and they place great demands on themselves and on others. Unless they can temper this through therapy and/or a metaphysical outlook, they might be better off leaving the acting profession and becoming drama critics.

Fear of Inadequacy

This fear seems to imply that the actor has a strong inferiority complex, yet in many cases nothing could be further from the truth. In order to feel inadequate at an audition, one must have a strong feeling of what being "adequate" is really like. The actor feels that he or she is not living up to his or her high standards. The cure is to give oneself reason to feel adequate at the audition. This would come from more rehearsal and a repetition of the performance/audition situation. The best place for this to happen is in a musical audition–performance technique class, where the audition is staged and rehearsed so that nothing was left to chance.

I must confess that for years I felt that my musical sight reading was terrible. It was true I was not a great sight reader, but I nurtured my feelings of inadequacy until they had mushroomed out of all proportion. When I think back now on all the shows I could have conducted, but turned down out of fear that I would look inadequate as a musician in front of instrumentalists in pit orchestras, I don't know whether to cry or laugh. What I never gave myself credit for was my ability to memorize a piece of music after reading it through twice. I concentrated on the weakness, not the strength. It really seems odd that the minute I accepted myself and my sight reading, the sight reading improved remarkably.

Inadequate Preparation

When this fear arises it is always because the actor or performer hasn't lived with the material long enough. In a show, the actor has at least three weeks to rehearse and learn the material before even previewing it. I am constantly amazed when actors wait until they get an audition, run out and quickly buy the sheet music to some song they think they can quickly learn, desperately beg some pianist or vocal coach to work with them, and then show up for the audition a few days later. It is no wonder they experience stage fright. They subconsciously realize that they are not prepared, and their own bodies, or rather their minds, are punishing them for their inadequate preparation. The remedy is simple. *Prepare in advance.* Don't wait until the last minute; learn and mount material before you will be required to audition. Learning to prepare is a skill that can be easily taught. I literally teach my students the learning processes of song preparation, interpretation, and memorization. By the end of two or three weeks they can easily do it on their own.

Preoccupation with Self

This is the most common cause of stage fright and the most easily remedied. The attention of the performer is centered on himself, on how he sounds to himself, on how he is moving, on what he is doing with his hands, and on how he feels moment to moment. This is self-defeating because the only time our attention should be on how we are feeling is when we are sick. If we can take our attention from ourselves the voice will sing better, we will move better, our line readings will come out better, and we will feel better. How do we accomplish that? By placing our attention on an imaginary acting partner and playing a scene with and to them. The human mind can only concentrate on one thought or idea at a time, and it's better if your attention is on someone other than on yourself. In my performance classes we do definite spotting exercises that enable the actor to constantly focus on the acting partner. The minute this happens it is uncanny how quickly all nervousness and extraneous mannerisms disappear. I have accompanied some of the most famous performers in the world, and have never been nervous doing it because my attention has always been on accompanying them, not on listening to myself.

Being Placed in an Unfamiliar Role

The performer has studied the craft and technique of acting and feels secure when playing or hiding behind a character or role. All of a sudden at the audition the performer has switched roles. He or she is no longer an actor involved and immersed in character. He or she has suddenly become forced to take on the unfamiliar role of *entertainer*. Entertainers not only play to but feed directly off audiences. If they receive no love or laughter from their audiences, their performance goes down the tubes. This is not true of the actor, who should be able to give the *same* performance at a dress rehearsal or a run through, to a packed house or an empty one. The cure for this cause of stage fright is to reinforce the techniques that are familiar and that work for you. Remain an actor and don't become an entertainer at the audition. Again, the techniques outlined in this book and in good performance classes will help this along.

Fear of Failure

This is the most devastating fear of all, and one that really requires extensive therapy to work through. No one wants to fail, but failure is something that everyone has to experience at sometime or another. We become complacent about our successes, but we learn through our failures; a child learns to walk only by falling. Despite what you may believe, there is *always* a second chance. Our second chances are infinite as a matter of fact. Also, memories are very short, and failures aren't remembered for long in this business. If they were, Sondheim would never have written anything after *Anyone Can Whistle*, and *Carmen* would have died after its disastrous first performance in Paris. If you look at the audition as a "learning process," then the fear of failure wouldn't have that much power. To help rob it of power I always suggest to my students that they regularly "break in" material by auditioning for jobs they don't really want. That strips the audition of importance and makes it so much easier to audition for jobs you *do* want.

To sum it all up, stage fright is an unnecessary part of performing and auditioning. There is a vast difference between the mild anticipatory nervousness that is a healthy part of the performance process and shows you care enough to want to give it your best shot, and the debilitating paroxysms of fear that can immobilize a performer. It would be nice if we could all mature while we still have our youth and realize the truth of the Psalmist's words, "Vanity, vanity. Under the sun all is vanity." Although we may be the center of our own universes, when we finally realize that the sun will still rise and set even if we blow an audition, then we will no longer blow the audition. At least not from stage fright.

7

Sixteen Bars

There is nothing more frustrating for the actor at a musical audition than to be told that the auditors are only going to hear sixteen bars. When this happens, singers quickly thumb through their music to find the sixteen measures that show the strongest and most impressive part of their vocal range. Dancers also take this pretty much in stride because they are quite used to it; since the prerequisite for dancers looking to be hired for musicals is to show their dancing ability, which they usually do at a separate dance call, all that they have to do at this audition is prove that they can sing, which they can easily do within sixteen bars. The people who have the most to lose are actors who sing only passably. They usually wonder why they showed up to audition in the first place.

I think I can sum up the frustration that every performer must feel when this happens in a little ditty I wrote several years ago for a musical revue about auditioning that I somehow never finished writing. The lyric went something like this:

Sixteen bars!
They must be joking.
Only sixteen bars!

I gave up smoking,
Gave up coffee and switched to tea
Just to have some bastard make me belt up to a
     "B"
In only sixteen bars!
And then you're kissed off
After sixteen bars,
God! Am I pissed off.
After seven hours of waiting
It's a bit exasperating
Singing sixteen measly, lousy, stinking bars!

Thirty bucks for a vocal coach.
The pianist that I took was twenty more.
Then two long hours on a local coach
To Trenton, then a taxi just to get me to my door.
(etcetera)

These are all the lyrics that I can remember, and unfortunately they are no exaggeration. This sort of indignity awaits the auditioning actor all the time. Let's see if we can examine the causes of this syndrome and come up with some guidelines for handling it.

One of the major causes is simply, as I have stated over and over, that there are fewer and fewer shows and more and more performers. Gone forever are the days when you could take your pick of five or six musicals that were casting the same day, and casting directors had to sometimes *beg* actors to audition for them. I can remember, way back in the mid 1960s, earning a rather good living rushing from one theatre to another and from there to a rehearsal studio or two, accompanying actors, singers, and dancers for the countless auditions that were taking place every day. A good pianist then got $10.00 per audition and the same price for an hour of vocal coaching. Today, there isn't a pianist around who can earn a living by playing auditions alone. There are too few of them.

Not only are there too few musical auditions, at the few that do take place hundreds of performers are seen in the space of time that used to be alotted for thirty or forty. It seems ironic that the auditions that are being held today are about as crowded as our prisons and our schools, and for the same reason: economics.

Let's take a quick look at the expense of holding auditions these days. As of this writing, rehearsal studios that are large enough to hold auditions in and that are halfway decent start at $25 an hour. The rehearsal pianist is another $25 an hour. Add to this the cost of another room, if there is a simultaneous dance call, and we are talking about a daily expense in the neighborhood of $500 or more. If the show they are casting is an equity show then they are required to spend a minimum number of days holding EPIs (Equity Principal Interviews) before the actual auditions, which also involves renting audition space. If they are hearing people over the course of a week their expenses are already in the thousands.

When producers and directors are casting a show there is always the possibility that they may not see, and may miss, some fantastic talent. What do they do about it? You guessed it. They try to cram as many people as they can into one day of auditioning. Thus the rude admonition to those waiting to perform that they sing only sixteen bars. To add insult to injury, if they are really backed up they may cut that to eight bars.

How To Handle the Request

Obviously, if they ask you to sing sixteen bars you are going to have to comply, but *how* you comply is another matter. If you are a chorus type, by which I mean you are young, attractive, sing up a storm, and move well or even dance OK, then you ought to start off in a blockbuster, show-offy, razzle-dazzle piece approximately sixteen measures *before* your highest and strongest note (or notes). Chorus types are seldom used for principal roles, which hardly ever, even today, are cast from the chorus, so show them how handsome or pretty you are and how well you can sing. Chorus people are always hired because they sing and dance well and are attractive to look at on stage.

On the other hand, if you are an actor or actress who sings and you want to be considered for a principal role, the auditors may not be impressed by your voice, adequate as it is for an actor, when they have already heard great voices coming from chorus people. What you must do is show them that you can act in song. You will, I hope, have with you a number that has been completely staged by you, one that shows off your ability to act a lyric. Disregard their request to hear only sixteen bars. Start at the *beginning* of the number, verse and all. Let them stop you. Do not let the pianist take on that decision; be sure to tell him that you are taking it from the top and that he is to play until they (the people auditioning you) instruct you to stop.

If they do not listen to the whole song and they interrupt your performance you have lost nothing. They would not have been interested in you for that particular show anyway. However, it has been my experience that if your performance is interesting and you are a good actor/singer, who is even remotely right for that role, they will not stop you. Even if they can't use you for that particular show it is possible that you will get a callback for some other show one of them is connected with. A good audition and a good performer *will* be remembered. I have seen countless actors that I have coached and played for get jobs in shows they never auditioned for originally, or get hired later to replace the person who did land the part months after they originally auditioned.

I will never forget seeing this happen to Penny Fuller, who got the coveted role of Eve Harrington in the Broadway musical *Applause.* I played her original audition, which was brilliant, but someone else got it. That someone else was dismissed out of town and Penny was called in to replace her. The rest is history. Penny was subsequently nominated for a Tony Award as best supporting actress in a musical. She was a knockout as Eve Harrington.

The important thing for dancers and singer/dancers to bear in mind when auditioning is that even though they may have become used to preparing a sixteen-bar segment of a song that shows their highest and strongest notes, if they are called back they will be expected to give a credible performance of an entire number. Now is the time to change that tired-out repertoire of songs that everyone else has run into the ground. The list of songs in Chapter 13 will give you some suggestions that might be just right for you.

At this time I should mention one major reason that a well-known casting agent of my acquaintance thinks is responsible for the sixteen-bar syndrome. As he puts it, "They just stand there for an entire song with their hands at their sides. . . . They look like department-store dummies. Their eyes are constantly turning in their heads, completely unfocused. After seven or eight measures I know all I need to know about them!"

If you fall into this category then you desperately need to reread this book and invest in a good performance and audition technique class, where you will learn how to use your eyes and your hands, to move, and to act a song as well. You can't get tomorrow's jobs with yesterday's skills and you certainly cannot get them with no skills at all.

8

Please Don't Shoot the Piano Player!

Of all symbiotic relationships, there is probably none as misunderstood as that between the actor/singer and his accompanist.

Just stand outside any studio where musical auditions are taking place. If there are grimaces of pain etched on the faces of those who have just auditioned, you can tell that the pianist was absolutely the worst. Of course this is a signal for the next victim to anticipate a fate akin to being stretched on the rack or boiled in oil. On the other hand, if the accompanist is good, the singers may exit with smiles and reassure those waiting to perform that this is their lucky day.

What is this power and mystique that a pianist possesses? Why are actors so intimidated by accompanists that they treat them either with extreme reverence or extreme contempt?

Part of the answer lies in the fact that the large majority of actors and singers do not read music. They cannot make sense of those little notes, clefs, stems, and rests that clutter the page. In their minds anyone who can is worthy of the kind of respect reserved for a rabbi who has mastered and can translate the Caballah. And it is a simple law of dynamics that one takes away from one's feelings of self-worth when elevating another onto an undeserved pedestal. It is the pianist's job to know how to read music and make sense out of all those hieroglyphics, not yours. Do you berate yourself for not knowing how to cut up a side of beef like your butcher can? Certainly not! So let's strip away those false illusions about the divinity of accompanists once and for all, and face some salient facts.

First of all, the best accompanists are not always the best sight readers. Good sight readers may be able to play exactly what's written on the page, but can they embellish it? Can they fill in what is missing? Can they transpose it into a more suitable key?

I am considered one of the best accompanists around, yet my sight reading is merely adequate. I am constantly reminded of an incident that occurred while I was still a student at Juilliard. Gus Schirmer, who was one of the top agents in New York City, heard me playing piano that summer at a resort restaurant and supper club in Southhampton, Long Island. He called to ask if I could accompany one of his star clients at an audition she had for the Broadway show *Bells Are Ringing*. He also asked me if I was familiar with the score. Naive, foolish me replied "Yes, I'm very familiar with it." After all, I had seen the show and had listened to the album. All of the hit tunes were in my repertoire.

I showed up early for the audition. The actress gave me the musical score. She was singing "Bonjour Tristesse Brassiere Company." The music was written in five sharps, in the key of B major, and I had never seen the music before. I attempted to struggle my way through it, but within sixteen measures the actress stopped and said to those assembled for the audition, "I'm sorry! I just can't perform for you with him playing." I wanted to die, or at least fall through the floor. Luckily for the actress the musical director was there, and he was familiar with the score. He accompanied her admirably. I slinked away and never (deservedly) got paid for the audition. Gus did, out of the kindness of his heart, send me students, and believe it or not he sent me out for other auditions.

That incident taught me one of the most powerful lessons of my life. From that moment on I studied and memorized almost the entire repertoire of the musical theatre. Never again did I leave anything to chance. By memorizing the music I could focus my attention on the actor/singer who was performing and anticipate every inflection and change of mood and tempo. I could also transpose whatever was required into any key that might be necessary.

I now have contempt for accompanists who do not at least try to become familiar with all the music they might be required to play. If they have chosen accompanying as a profession they had better be prepared.

A word about sheet music. Although the vocal scores of musical shows contain all the notes and accompaniment figures the composer and arranger intended, sheet music does not. Contrary to what most people believe, the accompaniment written on sheet music is *not* what the composer intended at all. Publishers print sheet music to sell copies, and music that looks difficult to play or read will not sell. Therefore, arrangers are hired to simplify the accompaniments so that anyone with a couple of years of piano lessons under his belt can play them.

These accompaniments do not enhance what a professional actor or singer has to offer. They are skeletal, to say the least. A good accompanist knows how to add the flesh that has been taken off the bones of the music. He or she knows how to make you sound good.

A good accompanist also knows how to follow and accompany the performer. Vladimir Horowitz and Van Cliburn may be brilliant pianists, but they never won any awards for accompanying someone. Accompanying is an art unto itself. It involves never overshadowing the singer; it involves using musical fills whenever the singer is holding a sustained note or pausing between lines of vocal text. There is a musical dialogue between accompanist and performer when they work optimally together. Therefore, it would be a good idea for you to learn a smattering of musical terminology so that a more perfect communication can take place.

9

Voice Teachers Versus Vocal Coaches

Time and time again I am asked the same question by actors who have decided that it is time to sing: What is the difference between a voice teacher and a vocal coach, and how do I go about selecting them? Most actors are confused, because if one were to judge by their titles, one could easily think they did the same thing. I have written on this subject in my "Audition Doctor" column quite frequently, and my views have changed considerably in the past few years, but let me get right to the point and first discuss voice teachers—what they do, what they shouldn't do, and how to find one that's right for you.

The Role of a Voice Teacher

A voice teacher trains, places, and exercises the voice in such a way that the student sings freely and healthily, and produces a free and honest sound. There!—I said it. This is what I think a voice teacher ought to do. God alone gives you a beautiful voice, not your voice teacher; but a good voice teacher *can* strengthen what you have been given and teach you to use it to best advantage.

Many voice teachers will tell you that they teach a "bel canto" vocal technique. *Bel canto*, in Italian, merely means "beautiful singing," so that is not the criterion one should use in selecting a voice teacher. As a matter of fact, how much money a voice teacher makes each week, how many students he or she has, and even how many famous people he or she knows is all unimportant and irrelevant. The only criteria in selecting a voice teacher are:

- How successful is the voice teacher in developing the voice without harming it, and

- How successful has the teacher been in training students who have succeeded as a result of studying with that particular teacher.

When I cast shows, or audition actor/singers here in New York, I usually ask those who sing freely and well who they study with. I invariably am given the names of the same six or seven voice teachers. But, and this a big but, do not make the mistake of thinking that because a particular voice teacher is in vogue he or she is the best one to study with. I know many inadequate teachers, who have actually harmed voices, who are busy teaching stars. A warm and captivating personality does not necessarily go with a good teacher, and people may flock to him or her because they are attracted to that teacher's nuturing personality.

The bond between a voice teacher and student is one of the closest bonds found anywhere. Indeed, when a student leaves prematurely you might think it was the end of a marriage or long-time love affair. Under favorable auspices it is more like a parent saying farewell to a child.

One must consider that a student will spend at least several years in studying, sometimes longer. Lessons can vary from once to, ideally, several times a week. Is it any wonder that the bond between student and teacher is close. Because the student must be vulnerable and open to the teacher, a parent/child relationship is more than likely to occur, and this can be damaging if the teacher is not a good one.

The primary danger of studying with a bad teacher is in permanently ruining the voice, or developing nodes on the vocal cords. A vocal cord (there are two) is a piece of cordal tissue that is from one half inch to five eighths of an inch in length. Through their opening and closing, the vocal cords resist and prevent the passage of air directed through them, which causes them to vibrate rather like a string vibrates when a violin bow is drawn across a string. At the same time, it is also similar to the way in which a reed or double reed instrument, such as the clarinet or oboe, is activated by the reed's vibrations as it resists the air blown through it. This makes the voice a sort of combination wind and stringed instrument.

Obviously, the vocal mechanism is delicate and irreplaceable and must be treated with care. Therefore, rule number one: *if it hurts, something's wrong!* Beware, beware the teacher who tells you the reason it hurts is that you are using muscles that you have never used before in a way you have never used them before. Singing should be a free and natural experience that eases tension rather than creates it. While the training process does require learning how to breathe and support your breath more efficiently, and that may lead you to use abdominal muscles in a new way, it does not mean that any pain, strain, or burning sensation should be felt in the vocal cords or throat. If singing is a painful experience for you, change teachers as quickly as possible. If you don't you run the risk of nodes on the vocal cords, which can easily put a singer permanently out of business.

I would also advise not studying with a voice teacher who does not develop *all* registers of the voice, especially if you are a woman. The female voice that does not use the lower or chest register is very much like a violin on which the lower G string is never played. It is limited. The literature of the musical theatre is quite demanding. One moment you are singing in chest, the next moment in head (soprano), if you are a woman. If you are a man, and you are doing ensemble work, expect to go from baritone to tenor and back again many times during the course of one show.

The reason many voice teachers do not develop the lower register is simple. They have never been taught to use it themselves, so how can they teach others? I know one very successful voice teacher who teaches her students to belt by telling them to scream. Yet she has a thriving clientele of students who don't know enough to leave and go elsewhere. I can't really blame her. She and others like her were conservatory trained for a career in opera, where the voice has to meet different requirements than in the musical theatre. In opera the voice has to sustain, for long periods of time, high notes that are usually sung on open vowels. This requires a vibrato, or tremolo, which may be an advantage when sustaining large-sounding notes on the stage of an opera house but is usually a disadvantage when singing in a musical, where the lyrics must be heard. Singers are hired for musicals mainly because they are articulate and can make sense of what they are singing.

So what are your alternatives? How can you ensure that the teacher you select will teach you to sing in your chest voice and develop the ability to belt? Quite simply, you can look for a voice teacher who can belt and sing in the lower register herself. Many voice teachers have had a Broadway career and have had to sing in all registers. Still others, including men (who obviously weren't created to belt), may very well have a superb knowledge of how to teach singers to develop the chest and belt voices. They also are excellent prospective teachers to study with.

Another thing a voice teacher should be able to teach you about is breathing. Breathing is one of the most misunderstood aspects of singing. It is not how you breathe but when you breathe, and how you use the breath, that is important. If breathing were the most import aspect of singing then all athletes would be Carusos. Athletes breathe to satisfy a greater-than-average need for oxygen by the cells and muscles of their bodies. This oxygen is delivered by the heart which under the demands of activity is pumping blood at several times its normal rate. Obviously an athlete has to breathe quickly and frequently to satisfy his or her needs for oxygen, and this involves using the muscles of the back and upper chest. Breathing this way allows runners to run quickly and does not interfere with the rhythmic pace such exercise requires. Dancers also fall into this category of shallow breathers. They breathe using their back muscles, and their abdominal muscles, which they use for support, are usually contracted. Singers are under none of the strain imposed on athletes or dancers. Their heart beat and pulse rate vary little when they are singing. They breathe not so much to satisfy oxygen requirements as to provide themselves with a supply of wind to activate the vocal cords and sustain a pure, open, and large sound. Abdominal breathing using the diaphragm as a bellows is what the singer employs, and it is this that he or she needs to learn how to do to sing properly.

I used to believe that in beginning voice study men should study with men and women should study with women, because the physiology of both voices is so different. Men have protruding Adam's apples and strong falsetto voices, which most women do not. Women, on the other hand, have chest or belt voices, which men do not. I used to feel that a student gained most initially from having a teacher who could do, and demonstrate what he or she was teaching. I have since changed my mind. I now think that the most important prerequisite is that the teacher be able to communicate fully, put the student at ease, and guide the student through the steps of producing open, free, clear, and honest tones.

The best way to find a good voice teacher is to ask people who sing well who they study with. Ask a lot of people, not just one or two. If the same name or names keep cropping up, you know that they bear investigating. There are a handful of teachers I recommend to my students because I have personally seen the results they have gotten. Do not be afraid to interview a teacher. You are not obligated to continue past the first lesson if it does not prove satisfactory. Your only obligation is to pay the teacher for his or her time.

When you work with a voice teacher, most likely your lesson will last thirty minutes. During this time you will be working on musical exercises or vocalises. These usually are performed on open vowel sounds, as these throat positions make it easiest to produce a sustained sound. Students eventually get bored singing nothing but exercises on open vowels, so it is inevitable that they will ask their voice teachers for songs to sing. Most likely the voice teacher will give them a classical Italian aria. So far, no harm done. If the teacher gives them a pop song, or some potboiler from the literature of the musical theatre, the student is in for some real trouble.

Enter the Vocal Coach

This is where the services of the vocal coach come in. Most voice teachers do not play the piano well. Many cannot accompany and almost none of them can transpose what they play into other keys. Their knowledge of the theatrical repertoire tends to be limited to the melodramatic and overdone standard songs that are around. The voice teacher is also so concerned with tone and vocal technique that performance values and lyrics necessarily suffer. Too many voice teachers admonish their students to ignore the consonants and "sing only on the vowel." This may do for a voice lesson where nothing but vocalises are sung, but it will certainly not do for the performance of a song. As I pointed out in Chapter 3, English is a language of consonants, compound consonants, dipthongs, tripthongs, and many other speech components. Songs are made up of lyrics which exist in poetic form. They make use of alliteration, onomatapoeia, and rhyme schemes. I may be prejudiced, but I think, like George Bernard Shaw, that English is the most expressive and most beautiful language in the world.

To quote from *Pygmalion*, "it is, after all, the language of Milton, of Shakespeare, of the Bible." It is also the language of W. S. Gilbert, Lorenz Hart, Cole Porter, Oscar Hammerstein II, Alan Jay Lerner, Fred Ebb, Stephen Sondheim, and all the other lyricists whose work you might sing. English vocal diction is something that most voice teachers not only don't teach but have no knowledge of themselves. I know: I teach many, many voice teachers. Teaching how to get across the diction is one of the many things a vocal coach should do, if he or she is any good.

The vocal coach should also pick out material that will not only enhance the singer but which will show the singer off to best advantage of auditions. Therefore the vocal coach needs to have a knowledge of and access to a huge collection of the musical theatre repertoire, encompassing the earliest shows and the latest offerings and reflecting all of the musical styles from operetta to rock.

The vocal coach's experience should include being conductor or musical director for off-Broadway musicals, or for summer stock or dinner theatre productions. The vocal coach may not be a strong singer himself, but he need to have a good understanding of the voice, where it lies, and how to get the most out of it through sensible musical phrasing and phrasing through the lyric.

The vocal coach should also be capable of teaching the performer where and how to move during the song, what to do with the hands and arms, and how to use the eyes. In short, the vocal coach should be an expert at teaching someone how to act while singing a song. In my classes, and in my private coaching, I teach a total performance technique including vocal diction, line readings, subtext, monologue, and complete use of the body as a dramatic instrument. The *only* thing I do not teach is voice. I have never claimed to be a voice teacher, and although I believe I know a lot about it I would never dream of monkeying around with someone's vocal apparatus. By the same token, I believe a voice teacher has no business working on songs without the same qualifications that a good coach has. Once a song has been learned incorrectly it is totally useless.

How does one find and pick a vocal coach? Here are some guidelines:

1. Ask around. Ask successful people especially who they work with.

2. Find out the background of your prospective coach. If he is jazz-oriented and interested in the nightclub scene, he may not be expert enough at what's going on in the musical theatre. If he is used to working with singers who use microphones, he may not know how to coach a singer who has to sing openly, fully, and legitimately at an audition for the musical theatre.

3. Satisfy yourself with your coach's ability as an accompanist. Can he play well enough for you at an audition? Can he transpose?

4. Very often you will be using accompanists provided for you by producers at most auditions. Your music will have to be written out in the key that's comfortable and correct for you. Will your coach write it out for you or send you to a copyist who will?

5. Make sure that your vocal coach has a knowledge of the working repertoire of the musical theatre. I would also ascertain that my prospective coach could pick out suitable material for me that wasn't overexposed at auditions.

6. Your vocal coach should be able to help you physically stage your songs so they look more like presentations than just readings. He or she should also be able to teach you what to do with your eyes and your arms during a song, and show you how and when to move.

7. Ask your voice teacher to recommend a good vocal coach. Just as I have ascertained which voice teachers get good

results and teach well by hearing singers sing, voice teachers know which coaches have gotten successful results with singers they have trained.

Be prepared to spend as much per hour for a coach as a voice teacher charges for a half-hour lesson. There are so many variations in the size of the fees both voice teachers and vocal coaches charge. Usually you get what you pay for, so it is worth the extra five or ten dollars an hour to study with someone really worthwhile. As I tell my students, "If you can get in five of my lessons what took ten with someone else, where's the saving?"

CHAPTER
10

Dressing for Success

Almost every profession has its own dress code. Bank presidents and Wall Street executives wear the same three-piece suits. Madison Avenue used to be synonymous with grey flannel. Policeman and fireman are readily identifiable by their attire, as are postmen, bartenders, waiters and waitresses, teachers, and blue-collar workers. Even preppies have their own unique and distinctive dress code.

It seems that, by and large, the only occupations to be immune from such requirements are those in the creative arts. Although writers are usually pictured in novels and in movies as wearing tweed jackets with patches on the elbows and a pipe sticking out of the left breast pocket, the only authors I know who dress this way are those who enjoy the affectation. And there really has not been a dress code for the working actor making rounds or going to auditions, except perhaps for a period in the late 1960s, when a style did arise that now spells death at any interview or audition.

In the 1960s almost every actor was into "the Method." Men wore old army fatigues and women dressed in clothing that looked like it had just come from a Salvation Army thrift shop. You could be ostracized if, God forbid, you were suntanned or (even worse) looked healthy. After all, if you were truly immersed in your craft you should be as pale and drawn as Barbra Streisand playing Yentl. I found it highly ironic that the minute most of these actors became gainfully employed their wardrobes changed for the better. As a matter of fact actors on Broadway always seemed to dress differently from their off-Broadway counterparts, and actors who really made it big and were imported to the West Coast would go out and invest in large, expensive wardrobes.

Today, there is little to differentiate the working attire of an actor from that worn by anyone else, with one exception—the chorus boy. For some reason, unknown to me, chorus boys all show up to auditions wearing the same faded denims, the same running shoes, the same sweat shirts, and the same two days' growth of beard. It is true that chorus people work harder than anyone else in the business, and it is also true that when performing, especially at a dance call, they need to dress in a way that will give them complete freedom, but there has to be a better way. Usually at dance calls there are dressing rooms where they can change into leotards, and since dancers don't usually walk the streets in leotards they can afford to dress in a more pulled-together look.

The issue of what one wears is an important one, primarily because throughout history all class and caste distinctions have been based at least in part upon the superficial impressions made by clothing. It is no different in an audition situation, and that is why I want to offer a few guidelines for attire and appearance here.

Avoid Casual Attire

No matter how you slice it, an audition is a business interview, and that superficial first impression they get of you must be a good one. As a matter of fact it has to be the *best* one. At all interviews and auditions you should strive for a pulled-together look that reflects how you want them to believe you feel about yourself. I honestly think that subconsciously we dress for others in direct proportion to our feelings of self-worth, at least in the business world. Doesn't it seem likely that these feelings of self-worth will be reflected in the job offers we get, and in the amount of our weekly paycheck?

A good rule of thumb in dressing for auditions and interviews is to dress as if you were meeting an important director or agent at a good restaurant. I always tell my students, "Pretend you're meeting them for drinks at Sardi's." Dress UP for the occasion.

Dress To Enhance Your Personality

If a picture is worth a thousand words, then one's attire is worth at least as much, if not more. The psychology of color is so widely known, and there are so many excellent books out on the subject, that I do not have to go into it in detail here. We all know that colors have their own implications. Doesn't one wear black to a funeral, or if one is in mourning? Didn't Hester Prynne sport a scarlet letter "A"? Don't we associate white with purity and innocence and earth colors with honesty and down-to-earthness? We tend to trust people who wear brown. We find midnight blue, and people who wear it, sophisticated. Narrow pinstripes suggest successful businessmen. Wide pinstripes can suggest members of organized crime.

Red is such a dynamic color that it enfuses those who wear it with a feeling of intense energy or aggressiveness. Yellow is sunny; turquoise, sharp and cool. Pink and lavender are refined, gentle, and romantic. Blue pastel shades evoke a quiet honesty. Checks and plaids are associated with a robust, outdoorsy quality. Paisley tends to impart a more refined, laid-back image. Primary colors are bold and hot; pastel shades are cooler and dreamier. The list is endless.

Although there are many books out on the subject of how to

dress using the psychology of color, the important thing to keep in mind while reading them is that you want to dress in a way that projects your personality and amplifies your strengths, while minimizing your defects and weaknesses. Most of these books are written with the business person in mind. If you are an actor and will NOT be playing a businessman or woman, don't dress that way.

Wear the Right Shoes

Feet are so important to the actor that footlights were the first theatrical lighting to evolve. Feet are the first thing to be looked at in an audition or interview. Especially when an actor makes an entrance. After all, we "look a person up and down" rather than down and up.

One man whose name escapes me thought shoes were so important that he left his fortune to Actors Equity Association, to set up a fund to provide shoes for actors so they could make rounds without ever having to look "down at the heels."

Proper shoes are not only attractive to the eyes, but they allow the actor to walk naturally without clomping or sliding the feet. Sneakers, running shoes, tennis shoes, and boots are not proper attire for any audition. Boots encapsulate the ankles, arch, and the rest of the foot, making it next to impossible to bend the ankle. People in boots make stomping noises which are bound to upstage them at a musical audition. They cannot help but walk with a swagger reminiscent of a grade-B western. Boots on women wearing skirts make these women look bottom heavy and destroy the aesthetic visual center of gravity.

Running shoes and sneakers rob the actor of the height that heels give. They also make casual what should be a formal occasion. Remember an audition is a total performance, not a first run-through.

The right shoes for men are dress oxfords or dress loafers with leather or rubber soles and heels; for women, comfortable heels that have some flexibility. No clogs or stilletos should be worn. On a typical wooden floor or stage, they will sound like cap pistols going off with each step.

Dress to Flatter Your Body Size and Type

If you have a weight problem, you should avoid wearing knits, which can accentuate the rolls of avoir du pois you are trying not to call attention to. If you are a man with spindly legs, this problem can be remedied by wearing pants that flare. Women with this problem should wear very light-colored stockings, rather than dark ones. Women with heavy legs should consider attractive pants or pants suits, but *only* those women having this problem should consider that alternative. Attractive legs are a fantastic asset on stage. Since stages are elevated to begin with, directors and producers are very finicky about looking at legs before they do anything else. Remember the cliché image of the producer with a cigar hanging out of his mouth, saying to the chorus girl, "Show me your legs, honey."

One more word about weight. Some of our most successful character actors have or have had weight problems. Jimmy Coco, Buddy Hackett, Jackie Gleason, Kaye Ballard, and myriads more owe part of their success to their rotundity. Proper attire will be flattering. The difference between portly and porcine is mostly a matter of dress.

Plan in Advance

Women will want to make careful use of makeup at an audition. Rehearsal studios are usually lit by fluorescent strips, and even with the light of day tend to give one a glary look. Judicious use of base and powder can soften the effects of such lighting. The audition on a stage, especially if it is under a worklight, places the performer either in front of a cavernous empty stage, or against voluminous black velour. Obviously at such an audition the actor should avoid wearing black and other dark colors, or he runs the risk of becoming invisible. Light colors are more appropriate for stage auditions, while darker colors would stand out more in front of the white-colored walls of a rehearsal studio. Also, I advise using eye makeup so that there will be some contrast and eyes will appear prominent in low light levels.

Don't Dress as Someone Else!

There are several schools of thought about dressing to suggest a period or a character at a musical audition. I personally think it works against the actor rather than for. Everyone showing up for that audition will have exactly the same idea, so you are going to see hordes of people wearing exactly the same get-up. No one is going to stand out except those who come dressed as themselves.

I recall, some years ago, playing auditions for several students at callbacks for the musical version of *Gone with the Wind*. All the women waiting to sing were wearing crinolines, or had their hair done up in curls à la Melanie or Scarlett O'Hara. The men were all wearing the same Edwardian jackets, even though they were off by a few years. Some of them had pasted on sideburns and moustaches to further enhance the period look. I had told my student not to dress in period but in the way that best reflected who she was, that highlighted her vivacious personality and that enhanced her physical features. Needless to say she was one of the few that got callbacks because she not only was good, but stood out in this group of period clones.

You may remember that brilliant audition scene in the movie *The Producers*, when Zero Mostel, Gene Wilder, and Chris Hewett are auditioning Hitlers for *Springtime for Hitler*. All the auditionees are dressed as Adolph Hitler except for Dick Shawn, who has shown up for the wrong audition. He naturally gets the lead.

You'll Perform Better When Dressed for It

When I was in high school I sat next to someone who not only graduated first in our class, but who wore his best suit whenever he took exams. He maintained that if he felt dressed up for it, he would do better, and he did. This and similar experiences have convinced me that most of us do act according to how we are dressed. Dressing up for an audition can give you a newfound confidence. If you look prosperous and successful, you are bound to feel prosperous and successful, and may very well end up that way.

Buy Clothes Wisely

A good working wardrobe does not have to be expensive. Actors living in large cities such as New York are indeed fortunate to be living in "fashion centers," where clothes can often be purchased at a little above manufacturers' cost. Even in the hinterlands there are mail order houses and department stores with annual and seasonal sales.

Think of your audition wardrobe as your working attire. You have to wear these clothes at interviews and auditions so make sure you buy clothing that can stand up to repeated laundering. Men will need a couple of pair of dress slacks, a few good shirts, some attractive ties, a good pair of dress oxfords or loafers, and a blazer or two. Turtle neck sweaters can serve as an alternative to dress shirts in the fall and winter. Women should have a couple of skirts and blouses, attractive hoisery, and two good pairs of dress shoes. Now, all of this does not have to cost a king's ransom. For what most of us are willing to spend on sports attire such as designer jeans and fancy running shoes, the average actor or actress can purchase a good part of a working wardrobe.

Keep a Diary

I recommend listing in your diary or appointment book exactly what you wear at each audition. The reason is simple. If you get a callback, many times they are not going to remember you by name or face, but what you wore and sang. If your audition is good, and you stand out above the other 70 to 100 people they see that day, why ruin the chemistry that was obviously working for you. Wear the same outfit, the same shoes, and wear your hair the same way.

Invest in Good Grooming

Don't be afraid to splurge on manicures and haircuts. Nothing makes a person look more unkempt, older, heavier, and out of sync than not being well-groomed. Pamper yourself so you can show agents and casting directors that you care about yourself. If you don't, they won't.

CHAPTER

11

Dancers Are Different

The hardest-working yet lowest-paid performers in the business have always been dancers. They start training at an earlier age than anyone else, and that training is much more vigorous than that of others in the business.

Usually it starts in one of two ways, either with classical training such as ballet, or else with tap, a more American discipline and concentration. A dancer who is interested in a career with a dance company or repertory group can look forward to endless classes and fatiguing hours of work at the barre. Those interested in musical theatre are required to be proficient in jazz, modern, and tap as well as ballet. On top of this, any dancer aspiring to being in a musical has to be able to do one more thing—sing.

Most dancers find musical auditions much more difficult than most actors, not because they do not have the talent for them, but because they face more problems in singing and need to take a different approach in their training. This of course is a generalization, but I have found it to be true after twenty-five years of coaching dancers as well as actor/singers.

If you are a dancer, one of the most important facets of your vocal training will be learning how to breathe so you can support tone and take in a steady supply of air to vibrate your vocal cords. Dancers breathe much differently than other people. They breathe like other athletes, especially runners, do. They have to sneak quick breaths and because they are in motion these breaths tend to be shallow ones; they also use their back muscles instead of their diaphragms. Perhaps the reason for this is that the diaphragm and abdominal muscles are most often in a state of tension while one is dancing. Because most active dancers are shallow breathers they may experience problems, especially in the beginning of their vocal training, in sustaining pitch.

Another difficulty that many dancers face in singing a song is an overwhelming self-consciousness that makes the musical audition situation for them truly a living nightmare. I believe this comes from the fact that dancers express themselves physically and not verbally. I also believe that this is why they quite naturally gravitated to an emotionally expressive art form like dance in the first place.

To overcome self-consciousness and shyness, dancers need to enroll in a good acting class and learn how to communicate verbally as well as physically. Joining a musical performance class is the very next step they should take in becoming articulate, in learning to make a song come to life, and in gaining confidence in an audition situation.

Most dancers are in awe of anyone who can sing well, and this sometimes gets them into trouble when it comes to choosing a voice teacher. Dancers tend to be too easily impressed with the wrong credentials in that they may pick teachers who boast of operatic experience without determining whether the teacher understands the demands of the musical theatre and can help them develop a free and honest voice that is right for them.

When it comes to selecting audition material, dancers need numbers that are quite different from those suitable for their actor/singer counterparts. While actor/singers audition for directors and musical directors first and for choreographers second (they are required only to be able to move), dancers audition for choreographers first and are hardly ever seen by the director during the audition process. The primary requirements for dancers is their dancing ability. If they can sing, it is icing on the cake and it means they can do chorus work as well.

Usually, dancers will never be asked for more than sixteen bars that show off the belt or chest voice. Very rarely will they need to show off the soprano or head voice as well. That is why it is important to choose a voice teacher who can develop the belt, if you have it, or at least the chest as well as the head voice.

The best audition numbers for dancers are up-tunes where the lyric moves very quickly. The more words coming out of you in a given measure, the less empty space (air) that you will have to fill with acting beats. Ballads leave a performer more vulnerable than up-numbers, in that they require greater acting ability to fill the vast emptiness of held, sustained notes and rests.

The best way to find good audition material is to either work with a vocal coach who understands the needs of dancers or to listen to the original cast albums of shows that starred dancers and choose material from them. If you are a man, investigate the shows that starred Harold Lang, such as *Pal Joey* and *Look Ma I'm Dancing.* If you are a woman, Gwen Verdon shows, such as *New Girl in Town, Red Head,* and *Sweet Charity,* will have suitable audition songs. I have also included a list of songs that are especially effective for dancers in Chapter 13 of this book.

12

Tactics for Survival

Charles Darwin may be right about "survival of the fittest" in the animal world, but in the world of the actor/singer we are better off changing that to "survival of the smartest." It takes brains, not brawn, to make it in the highly competitive world of the theatre and even more so to survive in the musical theatre.

Making it in our business requires several things. First of all, you have to have the "smarts," that instinctual knowledge of how to keep up with or surpass your competition and which includes knowing who can help you and how to get them to do it. You must have a realistic knowledge of what you can and can't do and a sense of your own self-worth. Survival also requires a sense of humor about our place in the divine scheme of things—a true belief that we are evolving, always becoming something better than we were before. I've never met a successful performer who didn't believe in a power greater than himself. It is not within the scope of this book to teach you how to acquire this or to preach a metaphysical approach to life. All I can do is share my practical experiences with you. The first is all about getting seen.

Getting to be seen by an agent is one of the most difficult things a performer can accomplish. Agents today refuse to see potential clients because Actors Equity Association, some years ago, determined that agents should not be allowed to collect a commission on jobs paying minimum scale. Since this encompasses the majority of work available for actors, agents are rightfully reluctant to submit actors for jobs from which the agent will never see a penny. If an agent does sign a client who has little previous experience, it is usually only because the agent is willing to invest the time and expense in nurturing that client so that he or she can become a salable commodity for roles that pay above scale, or so that the agent can realize a commission from TV commercials, soaps, and film.

Setting up an appointment with an agent is a real coup. Singing for one is a rarity. Getting a chance to be interviewed just for consideration to audition requires a wait of many hours, and, if you are lucky, you might be allowed to sing eight to sixteen bars of a song, which is the norm these days.

How then does one get to see an agent or casting director? Well, it takes a little thought and some imagination, but it can be done. Agents are constantly barraged with pictures and resumés, and all the ones I am familiar with will not take calls from actors they do not know or do not wish to know. Here are some suggestions for getting an agent to want to know you that I've given to a number of my students and which seem to have worked for them.

1. Invite them to lunch. After all, agents do have to eat. I don't know anyone who will turn down a free lunch, and you certainly will make a better impression in more relaxed surroundings, especially when you are giving something first before asking for something in return. Write a clever little note with a standing invitation. It will *not* go into the wastebasket. I promise you.

2. Try to become friendly with someone who works for the agent. Receptionists and secretaries can be helpful in making sure that your resumé is the one that gets seen and doesn't get discarded.

3. Try sending amusing greeting cards. Do anything that reinforces the fact that you exist and that you are an entity who is thoughtfully inventive and available.

Clever gifts can do wonders. I once had a student who tried for many weeks to get one of the top Broadway directors to consider her for a part in a straight play that already was having a long successful run. She found out that he had a sweet tooth. On my advice she went to Dumas, one of New York's most expensive and prestigious pattiseries, and bought a generous slab of triple rich chocolate-cream layer cake. She wrapped it in Saran wrap, put it in a nest of tissue paper in a very expensive-looking silver gilt gift box, and enclosed a note reading: "You really should meet me and let me audition for you. I think I'm your Piece of Cake!" Not only did she get the audition; she got the job. By the way, secretaries may open the boss's mail but I don't know one that will dare open a gift marked "personal."

After getting in to see an agent, the next most difficult accomplishment is getting an agent, casting director, producer, or even a reviewer to come and see you. There is nothing on this earth more frustrating than not having people know what it is that you have to offer, especially when you are appearing in something that you are proud to have the world know about.

Every actor, singer, dancer, and entertainer eventually appears in some showcase, revue, play, or nightclub act, at which time they face the prospect of letting people know who they are and where they are. There isn't one of us who doesn't have his or her mailbox cluttered with flyers or postcards announcing someone's appearance in something or other. If it is a showcase production we may mark it on our calendar since the three or four dollars it costs for admission are not usually going to bankrupt us. After all, we'd spend more than that on a movie. A nightclub appearance is another thing entirely. There is usually a cover charge that varies from five to ten dollars, plus a minimum charge of five or six dollars that has to be spent on drinks or, if you're lucky, on food.

I don't drink (and there is no way that I can consume six dollars' worth of Perrier or Tab), so the $16.00 that I have to spend to see someone I know in a nightclub act is not money I spend indiscriminately. Those people had better be pretty important to me for me to make the effort to see them.

The actor appearing in a nightclub act is going to have a very tricky time getting people to come see him or her. After all, your good friends will see you once, but how do you get those that you only know casually, or not at all, to come in and watch you strut your stuff? The answer is publicity.

Many actors work as their own publicists and press agents. They design their own postcards and flyers if they have an artistic bent. If they don't they can enlist the aid of artistic friends who may create an impressive flyer usually with the aid of Presstype, available at any stationery store, which gives a professional look to the lettering. They compile mailing lists of everyone they have ever met, and they go through the Ross Reports,* which list everyone in show business, and send flyers to every agent in town. This, however, is not enough. Most of the people that performers need to have see them are so barraged with these things that they will simply throw them in the wastebasket. Here's where the services of a good publicist/press agent come in.

Your first reaction is going to be, "I can't possibly afford it." My answer is, "You can't possibly afford not to." When you think of the hours, really days and weeks, of rehearsals that you have put in, and the cost of the vocal coach and pianist that you have had to hire, you must realize that it all goes down the drain if the right people do not come to see you.

Most press agents are not working all the time. Although it is true that press agents belong to an association (ATPAM) and that there are specific minimum rates for Broadway and off-

---

*These are available at any drama bookstore.

Broadway shows, publicists are free to charge whatever they wish for individual clients. If they like you and believe in your talent there is no reason they wouldn't work out a deal with you in exchange for a commitment for future work when you are in the position to afford it. There are no free lunches in any business, though, so be prepared to pay what you can reasonably afford.

I once needed the services of a press agent for a show I had put together to showcase my students. I got in touch with a marvelous lady who offered to be our press agent for a very modest fee with the understanding that should the show move and become successful she would receive a percentage or regular fee. She encouraged me to write to the critics who knew my work and invite them to see the show. Those critics I didn't know were invited directly by her. She set up four radio interviews within a one-week period. She suggested many important, viable ways of getting in touch with people. I had impressive invitations printed, the same kind that you receive for weddings, and these are not the sort of invitations that wind up in the garbage. A student of mine designed them and my press agent wrote the copy for them.

She called all the accessible critics in town who reviewed nightclubs and cabaret, and sent them press releases that she had written. *They came.* Having a press agent really boosts one's standing and can offer an air of legitimacy to a request to be reviewed. And although having critics come to review you can be a two-edged sword—there is no way to predict what they will like and what they will dislike—even if you get a negative review people will at least know where you are appearing.

What a good review does is to bring the public in. It also will be a deciding factor in bringing in all the agents and casting directors that you want to be seen by.

To sum it all up: Even if you are in the right club or the right showcase, you need outside help to let the world know you are there. It is one thing to let people know where you are and another thing to get them to want to come. For this you definitely need a press agent. To find one, either look in the Ross Reports or write or phone Celebrity Service Incorporated in New York City for a listing.*

Up until now we have discussed tactics that will get us seen or get us known. There are also tactics that require certain attitudes that *must* be cultivated if we are to keep and earn the success that we so desperately desire. Like it or not, we live in a universe that is orderly, and one that operates through some logical metaphysical laws. There is no way we can begrudge others their success and have success come to us at the same time. In some way what we wish for others is what we attract to ourselves. The story of the despicable Eve Harrington in *All About Eve* is all too real. We have all known Eve Harringtons in our lifetimes and we have nearly always seen them get back what they gave.

One of the most important "tactics" you need to develop in order to survive in show business is gratitude. Blanche Dubois is not the only one who has had to rely on the "kindness of strangers." As a matter of fact, there probably isn't a soul in our business who hasn't received something good from another person, without anything expected in return. There is nothing that can nip an actor's career in the bud as quickly or as potently as ingratitude. This may seem a strange subject to be writing about, especially in a chapter entitled "Tactics for Survival," but several negative experiences and many positive ones have made me do some hard thinking, and I have decided that it is a topic that bears writing about.

One of these experiences had to do with two former students of mine. One was a woman I had worked with for three or four years. I believed in her talent to such an extent that I obtained two nightclub engagements for her and accompanied her myself. I also hired her, in my capacity as director, to be presented at the Citicorp Center in New York City, in a "Stars of Tomorrow"

Celebrity Service Inc., 171 West 57th Street, New York, New York 10019. (212) 757-7979.

program that the American Guild of Variety Artists (AGVA) created to help launch new talent. I wanted her to get the best training possible, and because she couldn't afford the tuition, I gave her a scholarship so she could take my performance classes free of charge. All she had to do in exchange was take attendance and make sure that the students in the class were paid up. One night she simply didn't bother showing up for class, nor did she phone to say she wasn't coming. I had to call her in order to get my class enrollment book and money receipt book back.

The other ex-student was one I hardly knew at all. We met because I prepared him for an important audition for a Hollywood Bowl concert which he easily got. He had a phenomenal voice, and like my female student I hired him, and not only presented him at the Citicorp Center but featured him at one of my demonstration lectures before a packed house where there were several important agents in the audience. He also was on full scholarship and was studying with me free of charge. Right after the demonstration–lecture he disappeared. I never received a thank you note or a call from him.

Now, I was not bitter, but I was hurt. I have been around long enough to realize we do things for others because we want to, not for the thanks that we hope to get, *but*, and this is a big but, we do not have to continue doing favors for ungrateful people.

My two former students have lost out because I will never hire them or suggest them for anything that I am casting or connected with. This is not out of bitterness, but because I realize that they can never be an asset to any production when there is no sense of gratitude, loyalty, or commitment. Could you imagine what might happen if one night they didn't feel like showing up to perform?

What can gratitude accomplish? A simple thank you note can work wonders if it is a sincere one. It can even get you a job. I would now like to share one of my most exciting experiences with you. It happened when I had completed my first year of graduate work at Juilliard. My idol had always been Richard Rodgers; I worshipped his music and knew almost everything he had ever written. It had been announced that Juilliard was going to bestow the very first Rodgers and Hammerstein award to a composer for the musical theatre at their May commencement. I didn't think I had a chance. I received a note from William Schumann, who was then the president of Juilliard, telling me to show up for commencement because I had won the Freshl award for writing the best art song.

I really didn't want to show up for the commencement exercises because, I am ashamed to admit, I couldn't bear the thought of watching someone else win the Rodgers and Hammerstein award that I so desperately wanted. Miracle of miracles, my name was called and I became the very first recipient of that award.

It took a lot of soul-searching before I could write the thank you note I wanted to write to Richard Rodgers. It was easy to thank Juilliard and William Schumann, but not Richard Rodgers. I was afraid that if I wrote he might think I wanted something from him and he might resent my letter or reject me by not answering. I finally decided that I had to write and tell him how much I loved his music, how proud I was to receive the award he had set up, and how grateful I was to him for making it possible for me to win it. Since it was all true, the letter was an easy one to write. I felt so much better after sending it.

Less than a week later I received a telegram inviting me to an interview with the great man himself. I played him some of my music and before that afternoon was over I was signed to an exclusive publishing contract with an advance of several thousand dollars, a tidy fortune in those days. All this happened because I wrote an honest, heartfelt thank you letter.

Why is gratitude so necessary if one wants to succeed? Maybe it's because all human beings have a need to be stroked as well as to stroke others. We all have the need for honest appreciation. Perhaps that is one of the reasons so many actors hold on to faded press clippings, and look forward to good notices with such anticipation. They need to know that their work was, and is, appreciated. Earned praise is certainly the most powerful teaching tool there is in the universe. It is the basis for all forms of training, and it is the basis on which I teach my students and my classes.

When was the last time you thanked an agent for submitting you, even if you didn't get the job? How long has it been since you contacted the teacher who helped and believed in you, just to say "I'm thinking of you"? Did you ever send a card to anyone who helped further your career? What about the casting director who leveled with you and told you the things you needed to hear, even if they were unpleasant? Do you ever remember to thank people that you worked with for their former kindnesses?

When we are young, attractive, and vivacious it is easy to believe that the world revolves around us and that people should be only too eager to help us, lucky that they have an opportunity to do so. Maybe we have been spoiled by our parents and families and haven't yet learned that giving is not the norm for an impersonal society. Before we grow old, the greatest thing we can cultivate is a posture of gratitude.

Gratitude is remembered for a long, long time after it is expressed. It makes your benefactor want to befriend you over and over again. If it is genuine, appreciation can create a feeling of happiness so intense that it makes the recipient flourish like a freshly watered garden. It is one of the finest gifts you can give someone, and it comes back to you a hundredfold.

CHAPTER

13

A Compendium of Audition Songs

In compiling this list of more than 130 songs suitable for audition and performance purposes, I strenuously avoided songs that are overdone or improper for the particular use we are concerned with. The list reflects only examples of my own personal taste in audition material, and it is by no means exhaustive. It will, however, give you an excellent head start in selecting songs that are right for your particular situation and that will help showcase your talents to best advantage.

The songs are listed under the following headings: Juvenile (male and female), ages 7 through 13; Juvenile (male and female), ages 14 through 20; Romantic Lead (male and female); Character Actors (male and female), ages 21 through 40; Character Actors (male and female), ages 40+; Belt Songs; Songs for Dancers; Songs for Singers; and Comedy Songs.

The age range for Juveniles may vary. Many actors look much younger than they really are, and it is the age that one projects rather than the age one is that determines the age range one can audition for. This is especially true in casting adolescents. Very often, actors in their twenties—sometimes those approaching their thirties—are cast to play teenagers because they are more right for these roles than younger actors. Use your judgment in realistically typing yourself.

Romantic Leads are usually in their twenties through forties, depending upon the requirements of the songs and book of the musical in question. Curly and Laurey in *Oklahoma!* are obviously in their early twenties, as are Julie and Carrie in *Carousel*. Billy Bigelow from the same show could be in his thirties, yet Gittel in *Seesaw*, based on the play *Two for the Seesaw*, would be in her late thirties. There are wide latitudes in the age range of romantic leads. When I think it is necessary, I try to list age restrictions in the "comments" section that follows each song.

Character Parts are usually played by actors who either have secondary roles (the guy who doesn't get the girl, or the girl who doesn't get the guy) or who may provide comic relief. Examples of character parts strongly featured in the musical *Oklahoma!* would be Ado Annie, Will Parker, and Ali Hakim, representing the younger and more comic character type; Jud Fry, representing the more serious character type; and Aunt Eller, representing the older character type.

I have compiled a representative list of Belt Songs only because women are very often asked to bring one in. Although almost any woman's song, especially up-numbers, can be belted, many would sound ludicrous if sung that way. Imagine "I Could Have Danced All Night" or "Wouldn't It Be Loverly" being belted? It would do nothing for the performer and certainly wouldn't do much for the song. In the other categories of types and songs that are listed, I indicate if a particular song can be belted. Check the "comments" section. If the words "belt," or "can be belted" appear, by all means feel free to use that particular song as a belt number.

I have already discussed the fact that dancers are different and require different types of material (Chapter 11). Therefore, I have also included a list of songs suitable for dancers to sing at vocal auditions.

There is no reason why singers should not be able to show off their beautiful and rich voices, which is why I have included a section of songs that will allow you to do just that. I have tried to include gorgeous songs by the best composers available, Kern, Rodgers, Gershwin, Berlin, Arlin, Styne, and others of equal gifts. These songs require more vocal technique, range, and sustaining power than do songs for actors and dancers.

The last category of songs I list is Comedy Songs. Please refer to Chapter 5, "How To Play a Comedy Song," for ideas on making these work.

One of the major difficulties in creating this list was that many of the original publishers may no longer own the copyrights and publishing rights to these songs. Since a number of the songs date from the late 1920s through the 1940s, and the original term of copyright (until a few years ago) was twenty-eight years, many of them have been assigned to new publishing companies. You can track these down by contacting ASCAP, the American Society of Composers, Authors, and Publishers, which has offices in New York, Los Angeles, and Nashville. Any songs and authors not listed in ASCAP's catalogue are probably listed in BMI's (Broadcast Music International), a company that has offices in the same cities as ASCAP.

If a song is out of print you can usually obtain a photocopy from the publisher at a very modest cost. In days gone by publishers usually gave music away to performers to get their material heard. Nowadays you'll have to pay for that same material. If you live in a major city there are libraries with huge collections, and all of them have Xerox machines. Although it is against the law to reproduce or copy a published work, I feel that if a publisher lets a work go out of print we are left with no alternative but to photocopy it if we want to use that work.

I must strongly advise you to resist the temptation to photocopy a work that is in print. You will be depriving the authors of their only source of making a living, namely, royalties. You will also be depriving the publisher of money necessary to amortize the original cost of publishing that work. The only reason that publishers allow works to go out of print is that it is not profitable to keep them in print. Xeroxing is one the surest ways to make it unprofitable.

Juvenile—Male and Female

AGES 7 THROUGH 13˙

Title, Author, Source & Publisher	Description & Comments
"Go Visit Your Grandmother" Kander & Ebb *Seventy Girls, Seventy* Sunbeam Music, a division of NY Times Music Corp.	Comedy up-number that is most effective when played directly to those auditioning you. Try to create comedy guilt trip.
"Be Kind to Your Parents" Harold Rome *Fanny* Chappell & Company	Comedy up-number
"Please Don't Send Me Down a Baby Brother" Fields & Schwartz *By the Beautiful Sea*	Great solo juvenile comedy number. Sheet music was never published. Take it off the original cast album.
"Little Lamb" Styne & Sondheim *Gypsy* Chappell & Company	Vulnerable ballad for young girl.

AGES 14 TO 18

(Male and female unless indicated otherwise)

"Love I Hear . . ." Sondheim *A Funny Thing Happened on the Way to the Forum* Chappell & Company	Best for young man 16 to 20. Comic possibilities. Wistful, charming.
"What Do You Think I Am" Martin & Blane	Good up-number for boy or girl. Age range 14 to 20 or so.
Best Foot Forward Chappell & Company	The mock anger or the lyric requires energy. Can be belted.

"Your Eyes Are Blue"
Sondheim
A Funny Thing . . .
Chappell & Company

Comedy ballad. Endearing & vulnerable. Was cut from the original show.

"It Might as Well Be Spring"
Rodgers & Hammerstein
State Fair
Williamson Music Inc.

Vulnerable ballad for young woman only.

"I Said Good Morning to the Sun"
Julie Styne, Comden & Green
A Party with Comden & Green
Chappell & Company

Manic comedy number. Up tempo.

"Your Good Morning"
Jerry Herman
Parade
Edwin H. Morris & Company

Charming medium tempo number for man or woman. Out of print.

"Boys and Girls Like You and Me"
Rodgers & Hammerstein
Williamson Music Inc.

Cut from *Carousel*. Recorded by Judy Garland from *Meet Me in St. Louis* but never used. Boy or girl.

"Little Boy Blues"
Hugh Martin and Ralph Blane
Look Ma I'm Dancing
Chappell & Company

Adolescent male medium tempo blues.

"Nine O' Clock"
Bob Merrill
Take Me Along
Chappell & Company

Perfect ballad for adolescent boy.

"I Hear Bells"
Shire & Maltby
Starting Here, Staring Now
Chappell & Company

Good semi up-number, better for young male.

Romantic Lead

(Male and female unless indicated otherwise)

"Have You Met Miss Jones"
Rodgers & Hart
I'd Rather Be Right
Chappell & Company

Effective slightly manic ballad for young man.

"My Romance"
Rodgers & Hart
Jumbo
Chappell & Company

Beautiful ballad for young man. Verse implies a man is singing it. Without the verse fine for young woman.

"You Are Never Away"
Rodgers & Hammerstein
Allegro
Williamson Music Inc.

Great up-number for high baritone.

"So Far"
(see above)

Beautiful ballad for man or woman.

"Like a God"
Rodgers & Hammerstein
Flower Drum Song
Williamson Music Inc.

Male up-number.

"I'm Your Girl"
Rodgers & Hammerstein
Me and Juliet
Williamson Music Inc.

Beautiful ballad for soprano.

"The Next Time It Happens"
Rodgers & Hammerstein
Pipe Dream
Williamson Music Inc.

Good up-number for soprano. Effective also as a belt number.

"Right as the Rain"
Harold Arlen & E.Y. Harburg
Bloomer Girl
Chappell & Company

Beautiful ballad for young man.

"I Wish It So"
Marc Blitzstein
Juno
Chappell & Company

Good legit dramatic ballad for soprano 20 to 40.

"Love Walked In"
Gershwin
Ziegfeld Follies
New World Music Corp.

Beautiful ballad, shows off voice. Male or female.

"Isn't It a Pity"
Gershwin
Pardon My English
New World Music Corp.

Medium tempo, witty, tuneful. Best for male. Good up-number for an actor.

"Dear Little Girl"
Gershwin
New World Music Corp.

Male up-number. Requires large range. High baritone or tenor.

"Something to Remember
  You By"
Dietz & Schwartz
Chappell & Company

Lyrical ballad, better for woman.

"I Don't Remember You"
Kander & Ebb
The Happy Time
Sunbeam Music Corp.

Wonderful dramatic ballad. Shows voice.

"Fifty Million Years Ago"
Schmidt & Jones
Celebration
Chappell & Company

Exciting up-number for man. Shows off voice.

"Long Ago"
David Henneker
Half a Sixpence
Chappell & Company

Beautiful sensitive ingenue ballad for young woman.

"It's a Nice Face"
Fields & Coleman
Sweet Charity (movie version)
Notable Music Corp.

Good ballad for either man or woman. Doesn't require too much voice.

"In the Still of the Night"
Porter
Rosalie
Chappell & Company

Beautiful song that shows off voice and sensitivity. Good for man or woman.

"Where Oh Where"
Porter
Out of This World
Chappell & Company

Up tempo waltz. Sophisticated lyric. For legitimate soprano voice only.

"That's for Me"
Rodgers & Hammerstein
State Fair
Williamson Music Inc.

Good actor's ballad for strong man.

"All Through the Day"
Jerome Kern & Johnny Mercer
Centennial Summer
Williamson Music Inc.

Gorgeous ballad for either man or woman.

"Up with the Lark"
(see above)
T. B. Harms Inc.

Charming waltz for woman.

"The Way You Look Tonight"
Jerome Kern
T.B. Harms Inc.

Good legit voice ballad for man. Romantic and lush.

"They Didn't Believe Me"
Jerome Kern &
   Herbert Reynolds
T.B. Harms Inc.

Beautiful ballad. Best for a man.

"Poor Little Hollywood Star"
Cy Coleman & Carolyn Leigh
Little Me
Valando Music

Legit soprano dramatic song. Requires extreme range. Goes to high B flat.

"Angelina"
Coleman & Leigh
Wildcat
Valando Music

Good actor's ballad. A personal favorite.

"One Day We Dance"
(see above)

Good slow waltz for either man or woman.

"Somebody Somewhere"
Frank Loesser
Most Happy Fellow
Frank Music Corp.

Perfect legitimate, soprano vulnerable ballad for ingenue.

"Make Someone Happy"
Julie Styne & Comden and
   Greene
Do Re Mi
Chappell & Company

Good audition ballad for man or woman.

"Fireworks"
(see above)

Exciting razzle-dazzle up-number for man or woman. Requires range and energy.

"Long Before I Knew You"
Julie Styne & Comden and
   Greene
Bells Are Ringing
Chappell & Company

Probably my favorite audition ballad. Perfectly constructed. Good for either man or woman.

"Ten Minutes Ago"
Rodgers & Hammerstein
Cinderella
Williamson Music Inc.

Good lilting waltz for young man or woman. Not too rangy.

"Do I Love You Because
You're Beautiful"
(see above)

Male ballad.

"You're Nearer"
Rodgers & Hart

One of the most beautiful ballads ever written. A perfect

Too Many Girls
Chappell & Company

Hart lyric. Man or woman, but better for a woman.

"Why Can't I"
Rodgers & Hart
Spring Is Here
Warner Bros. Music

Fantastic, vulernable yet sophisticated torch song for woman. Best in chest.

"Spring Is Here"
(see above)

Wonderful vulnerable legit soprano ballad.

"Small Town Boy"
Fred Silver
Fred Silver Songbook
Genesis III Music Corp.
distributed by Plymouth Music

Good ballad for young man with good high baritone.

"This Is My Last Show"
(see above)

Effective female ingenue ballad.

"Someone in My Life"
(see above)

Dramatic ballad. Rangy, requires a good voice.

"She Wasn't You"
Alan Jay Lerner &
   Burton Lane
*On a Clear Day You Can See
   Forever*
Chappell & Company

Great legit baritone audition song. Formal lyric (not in vernacular).

"Melinda"
(see above)

Good baritone ballad.

"What Did I Have That I
   Don't Have"
(see above)

Good chest or belt ballad for woman.

"Hurry, It's Lovely Up Here"
(see above)

Wonderful lilting charm song for ingenue.

"From This Day On"
Alan Jay Lerner and
    Frederick Loewe
Brigadoon
Chappell & Company

Great underdone ballad for man or woman. Lush, romantic, and rangy.

"One Promise Come True"
Michael Leonard and
    Herbert Martin
The Yearling
Edwin H. Morris & Company

Good up-tempo ingenue number.

"The Kind of Man a Woman Needs"
(see above)

Good chest torch song. Earthy. Better for 25–35 age range.

"I'm All Smiles"
(see above)

Great jazz waltz for either man or woman. Most often done by woman.

"Why Did I Choose You"
(see above)

One of the greatest ballads ever to come out of any show. Best for woman though man can sing it also.

"I'll Tell the Man in the Street"
Rodgers & Hart
I Married an Angel
Robbins Music Inc.

Perfect audition ballad for man or woman.

"You Are Too Beautiful"
Rodgers & Hart
Warner Bros. Music

Beautiful romantic ballad for romantic young man.

"Make the Man Love Me"
Arthur Schwartz &
    Dorothy Fields
A Tree Grows in Brooklyn
Chappell & Company

Perfect ingenue ballad.

"I'll Buy You a Star"
(see above)

Gorgeous male audition ballad. Requires good legit voice.

"Acorn in the Meadow"
Richard Adler and Jerry Ross
Almanac
Frank Music Corp.

One of the most beautiful ballads ever written for a black actor to sing. Harry Belafonte originally performed this. I strongly recommend it.

"There's a Room in My
    House"
John Kander, J. and
    B. Goldman
Family Affair
Subeam Music Inc.

One of my favorite ballads for a young leading man. Melody is exceptional. Larry Kent sang it originally.

Character Actors and Actresses

AGES 20 TO 45

"Could You Use Me"
Gershwin
Girl Crazy
New World Music Corp.

Good up-tempo manic, cutesy number for man.

"By Strauss"
Gershwin
The Show Is On
Chappell & Company

Good up waltz comedy number. Better for man. Play it like a Nazi.

"I Guess I'll Have To Change
    My Plan"
Dietz & Schwartz
Chappell & Company

Marvelous young "dirty old man" type of number.

"Way Out West on West End
Avenue"

Good comedy number, pseudo-western spoof, clever lyrics.

Rodgers & Hart
Babes in Arms
Williamson Music Inc.

Good for man or woman. Can be belted.

"Everything I've Got Belongs
  to You"
Rodgers & Hart
By Jupiter
Chappell & Company

Good chest or belt up-tempo for woman.

"Nobody Else but Me"
Kern & Hammerstein
Showboat (1936 version)
T.B. Harms Inc.

Good song for young male character actor who looks like he lacks self-confidence.

"I Have the Room Above"
(see above)

Romantic ballad for shy man.

"All I Need Is One Big Break"
Kander & Ebb
Flora the Red Menace
The Times Square Music
  Publications Company

Exciting up-number for young woman. Requires strong, rangy belt voice. A show stopper. Quite long, so must be cut.

"Can't You Do a Friend
  a Favor"
Rodgers & Hart
Harms Inc.

Touching short ballad for man or woman. Doesn't require much voice. Good acting piece.

"I've Got Five Dollars"
Rodgers & Hart
Harms Inc.

Brash up-number for young character actor.

"I'm in Love with the
  Honorable Mr. So and So"
Sam Coslow
Society Lawyer (movie)
Leo Feist Inc.

Torch song, more effective in chest for woman 20 to 35. "Other woman" type song.

"Summertime Love"
Frank Loesser
Green Willow
Frank Music Corp.

Good angry up-number for young man.

"Never Will I Marry"
(see above)

(see above)

Character Actors and Actresses

40 AND OVER

"Alone Too Long"
Dorothy Fields &
  Arthur Schwartz
By the Beautiful Sea
Chappell & Company

Beautiful ballad for man or woman.

"Happy Habit"
(see above)

Good character number for strong woman.

"I've Still Got My Health"
Cole Porter
Panama Hattie
Chappell & Company

Good strong comic belt number. Up-tempo for woman.

"More I Cannot Wish You"
Frank Loesser
Guys and Dolls
Frank Music Publishing Co.,
Inc.

Effective touching ballad for older man.

"I Never Know When To Say
  When"
Leory Anderson, Walter and
  Jean Kerr, and Joan Ford
Goldilocks
Mills Music Inc.

Good chest torch song for woman 30 to 50.

"Tomorrow Morning"
Kander & Ebb
The Happy Time
Sunbeam Music
Valando Music Corp.

Rascalish up-tempo for older man.

"Days Gone By"
Bock and Harnick
She Loves Me
Sunbeam Music
Valando Music Corp.

Nostalgic moving waltz for older man.

"Too Good for the Average Man"
Rodgers & Hart
On Your Toes
Chappell & Company

Comic character number with witty social commentary for man over forty.

"Be Happy"
Hal Hackady &
    Larry Grossman
Minnie's Boys
Sunbeam Music
Valando Music Corp.

Kurt Weill, Bertolt Brecht–type fatalistic song of advice for older woman.

"I'm Not a Well Man"
Harold Rome
I Can Get It for You Wholesale
Chappell & Company

Older man's song. A hypochondriac's complaint.

"Sew the Buttons On"
John Jennings
Riverwind
Frank Music Corp.

Good character song for mother type. Positive, Midwest unsophisticated.

"Oh, Diogenes"
Rodgers & Hart
Boys from Syracuse
Chappell & Company

Strong, earthy belt for strong woman.

"What Can You Do with a
  Man"
(see above)

(see above)

"Sing for Your Supper"
(see above)

(see above)

"Love Isn't Born"
Arthur Schwartz &
  Frank Loesser
Thank Your Lucky Stars
M. Witmark & Sons

Great number for earthy, mature character woman.

"The Springtime Cometh"
Sammy Fain & E. Y. Harburg
Flahooley
Chappell & Company

Charming nonsense song for character actor or actress. Stylized.

"Here's to Us"
Cy Coleman & Carolyn Leigh
Little Me
Edwin H. Morris

Strong show-tempo number for earthy, mature woman. Good belt number.

Belt Songs

"I'm All I've Got"
Milton Schaeffer &
  Ronny Graham
Bravo Giovanni
Mayfair Music Corp.

Good solid belt. Rangy, very fast.

"Put in a Package and Sold"
Nancy Ford & Gretchen Cryer
I'm Getting My Act Together . . .
Fiddleback Music Pub. Co. Inc.

Good solid, up, contemporary, pseudo-rock number. Emotional and theatrical.

"Nobody Does It Like Me"
Cy Coleman & Dorothy Fields
Seesaw
Notable Music Co., Inc.

Good earthy, solid belt.

"All of My Laughter"   Good up-number.
Albert Hague &
   Allen Sherman
Fig Leaves Are Falling
Playgoers Music Co., Inc.
Agent: Sam Fox Publishing Co.

"The Gentleman Is a Dope"   One of the best belt numbers
Rodgers & Hammerstein   around. Showy, dramatic.
Allegro
Williamson Music Inc.

"On the Other Side of the   Razzmatazz number. Showy.
   Tracks"   Best for younger woman.
Cy Coleman & Carolyn Leigh
Little Me
Edwin H. Morris & Company

"Wherever He Ain't"   Good fast belt for woman 20
Jerry Herman   to 40.
Mack and Mabel
Edwin H. Morris & Company

SONGS FOR DANCERS

(Male or female unless otherwise indicated)

"I Feel Merely Marvelous"   Up waltz. Chest register. For
Albert Hague & Dorothy Fields woman only.
Red Head
Chappell & Company

"Look Who's Dancing"   Up-number. Chest register.
Arthur Schwartz &   For woman only.
   Dorothy Fields
A Tree Grows in Brooklyn
T.B. Harms Inc.

"All I Need Now Is the Girl"
Julie Styne &
  Stephen Sondheim
Gypsy
Chappell & Company Inc.

Soft-shoe, production number. Man only.

"Your Eyes Are Blue"
Stephen Sondheim
(cut from *A Funny Thing Happened . . .*)
Chappell and Company

Charming vulnerable song perfect for adolescent. Doesn't require vocal ability.

"Ridin' on the Moon"
Harold Arlen
St. Louis Woman
Chappell and Company

Shows off voice. Up-number. Shows energy. Requires voice.

"Fascinating Rhythm"
Gershwin
Lady Be Good
New World Music Corp.

Good solid up-number for man or woman.

"Lady Be Good"
(see above)

Perfect medium tempo for male dancer. Not rangy.

"Do Do Do"
Gershwin
Oh Kay!
New World Music Corp.

Good up-number. Cute song for both male and female. Youthful vivacity.

" 'S Wonderful"
Gershwin
Funny Face
New World Music Corp.

Marvelous medium tempo number. Good for man. Not rangy, easy to sing.

"Love Is Sweeping the
  Country"
Gershwin
Of Thee I Sing
New World Publishing Corp.

Good solid, up, show tune. Great for either man or woman. Can be belted by woman.

"Of Thee I Sing"   Male up, requires strong voice.
(see above)

"Who Cares"   Charming song good for ei-
(see above)   ther man or woman.

"Nice Work If You Can Get It"   Good jazz up-tune.
Gershwin
Damsel in Distress
Gershwin Publishing Corp.

"Come Play Wiz Me"   Good song for sexy female
Stephen Sondheim   dancer with great body. Re-
Anyone Can Whistle   quires French accent.
Burthen Music Corp./Chappell

Comedy Songs

(Male and female unless otherwise indicated)

"The Shape of Things"   Good soprano comedy song.
Sheldon Harnick
The Littlest Revue
Saunders Publications Inc.

"The Twelve Days After   Soprano comedy song
   Christmas"
Frederick Silver
Belwin Mills

"Too Old To Die Young"   Black comedy number for
Murray Grand   woman over 40. Sophisticated
R.C. Jay Music Company   humor.

"We Can't Go on Meeting"   Sophisticated, fast, funny up-
Fred Silver   number for man 25–40.
Fred Silver Songbook
Genesis III Music Corp.
distributed by Plymouth Music
   Corp.

"True Confession"
Fred Silver
In Gay Company
Genesis III Music Corp.

Sophisticated song for woman.
Bitchy!

"I Said Good Morning to
the Sun"
André Previn and
Comden & Green
A Party With Comden & Green
Chappell & Company

Manic and hokey for man or
woman. Play it cornball.

"And Her Mother Came Too"
Ivor Novello &
Dione Titheridge
Chappell (London)

English comedy song for man.

"To Keep My Love Alive"
Rodgers & Hart
Connecticut Yankee
Warner Bros. Music

Sophisticated witty number
for woman. Soprano range but
can be transposed down if
necessary.

"I Love a Cop"
Bock & Harnick
Fiorello
Sunbeam Music

Good ingenue or young
character actress comedy
number.

"That Dirty Old Man"
Stephen Sondheim
A Funny Thing . . .
Burthen Music Corp.

Comedy number for older
woman or at least 35 plus. Requires strong chest and head
voice. Rangy. Shows off technique. Difficult!

"I've Still Got My Health"
Cole Porter
Chappell & Company

Funny earthy number for older
woman.

"Wait Till We're Sixty-Five"
Alan Jay Lerner &
Burton Lane
"On a Clear Day . . ."
Chappell & Company

Great comedy number for
older man. Up-jazz waltz.

"I Want To Be Bad"
De Sylva, Brown, and
    Henderson
Follow Through
Crawford Music

Naughty flapper number for brash young woman. There are unpublished racy lyrics you can take off the recording "De Sylva, Brown & Henderson Revisited," put out by Ben Bagley. It was sung by Blossom Dearie.

Index

About the Author

Fred Silver, one of New York's top vocal coaches, has worked with thousands of actors, including E.G. Marshall, Sandy Duncan, Nancy Dussault, Diane Ladd, Pat Hingle, Barbara Barrie, and Marsha Mason. For the past six years, he has written the "Audition Doctor" column for *Back Stage* magazine. Mr. Silver received Bachelor's and Masters' degrees from Juilliard, where he was awarded the first Rodgers and Hammerstein Scholarship for a composer of the musical theatre. He has written seven musical shows that have won more than fifteen ASCAP awards and a nomination for "Best Score" from the New York Drama Desk Circle. He was also musical director for both Upstairs at the Downstairs and Plaza 9 in New York City.